PERCEVAL
OR THE STORY OF THE GRAIL

CHRÉTIEN DE TROYES

A Translation into English by
A. S. KLINE

With Illustrations by
AUBREY VINCENT BEARDSLEY

POETRY IN TRANSLATION
www.poetryintranslation.com

Please direct sales or editorial enquiries to:
tonykline@poetryintranslation.com

This print edition is published by
Poetry In Translation (*www.poetryintranslation.com*),
via Amazon Services UK Limited (a UK limited company with registration number 03223028 and its registered office at 1 Principal Place, Worship Street, London, EC2A 2FA)

ISBN-13: 978-1090390691

CONTENTS

ABOUT THIS WORK

Chrétien de Troyes' Arthurian Romances, written in the late 12th-century, provide a vital link between the Classical Roman poets, Ovid in particular, and the later medieval world of Dante and Chaucer. The five major verse tales, namely Érec and Énide (c1170), Cligès (c1176), Yvain or the Knight of the Lion (before 1181) Lancelot or the Knight of the Cart (before 1181), and Perceval (before 1190), introduce motifs and plot elements that recur frequently in later literature. Well-structured, lively, and witty the tales were written for a sophisticated courtly audience, and the five stories considered together gave expression to the reality and the deeper ideals of French chivalry. Chrétien appears to have used themes culled from French and British sources, while characters such as Lancelot, and features such as the Holy Grail appear for the first time in European literature in his work. Here translated in rhyming couplets to mirror the original, rather than in unrepresentative prose, is a fresh treatment of one of France's and Europe's major poets.

LINES 1-68 CHRÉTIEN'S INTRODUCTION

HE little reaps who little sows,
And he who'd have good harvest knows
To sow his seeds in such a field
That they a hundredfold will yield;
For good seed in a barren place
Will shrivel there and fail apace.
Now Chrétien sows here the seed
From which a story will proceed,
And sows it in so good a place
Great profit shall his efforts grace,
For what he does is for the best
With whom the Roman Empire's blessed.
He is Philip, Count of Flanders,
Of greater worth than Alexander,
Of whom they give such good account.
For I will prove to you this Count
Is yet far better than the former;
For he amassed, that Alexander,
Vices within, and frailties,
From all of which the Count is free.
The Count is one who will not hear
Vile jokes, or suffer proud speech near;
And if one speaks ill of another,
Whoe'er it is, he's sad moreover.
The Count desires true justice, he
Loves Holy Church and loyalty,
At every baseness he doth groan;
He is more generous than is known,
Nor plays the cunning hypocrite,
But acts in line with Holy Writ.

'Let not thy left hand know,' it says,
'What thy right hand doeth, always.'
For he who receives is still aware,
And God, who lays our secrets bare,
And knows of all the hidden things
Within the heart, all its workings.
Holy Writ, why doth it command:
'Hide thy good deeds from thy left hand,'?
Because, according to the story,
The left hand signifies vainglory,
That's born of false hypocrisy.
The right? It stands for charity,
That boasts not of each good deed,
Seeks rather to hide them, indeed,
So that none know of it, but He
Whose name is God and Charity.
God is Charity, and who dwells
In Charity, and acts the Gospels,
Saint John says, I read with him,
'Dwelleth in God, and God in him'.
And know this then, of a verity,
Those gifts are gifts of charity
That good Count Philip doth give,
For naught counsels him so to live
But his own heart, frank, debonair,
Which teaches him to act the fair.
So is he not of greater worth
Than Alexander, who from birth
Nor charity nor good deed claim?
Yes, and no man doubts the same.
Thus Chrétien works not in vain,
Who's taken up his pen again,
To rhyme, at the Count's command,
The best tale that, in any land,
Did ever royal court regale.

It is the story of the Grail;
The book he has from the Count;
Judge how he renders his account.

LINES 69-154 THE WIDOW'S SON MEETS
A BAND OF ARMED KNIGHTS

When all the trees are blossoming,
The boughs in leaf, grass flourishing,
And the small birds, in their Latin,
Are sweetly singing, at their matins,
And all things are alight with joy,
There then arose the Widow's boy,
(She dwelt in the Forest Waste)
Saddled his horse, in eager haste,
And when he'd set his saddle there,
Upon his mount, took up, with care,
Three hunting spears and, all intent,
Forth, from his mother's house, he went.
He thought that he would go and see
The ploughmen she had there, whom she
Employed to plough and sow her land,
Six ploughs, twelve oxen there in hand.
Into the forest glade he pressed,
And the heart within his breast
Leapt, for the sweetness of the spring,
The small birds filling everything
With the joyfulness of their song;
All pleased him, as he rode along.
With the mildness of the weather,
He left his mount, free of its tether,
To graze, wherever they did pass
On the wealth of fresh green grass,

While he, skilled in hunting, cast
The spears he held, hard and fast,
All about him, on the forest floor,
Now behind him, and now before,
Now slanted low, now hurled high,
Till through the forest, by and by,
Five knights-in-arms he did hear,
In full armour, and passing near.
And a mighty noise they made,
Those riders in the forest glade,
For oft the branches of hornbeams,
And oak-trees, struck against, it seems,
The weapons, while the chain-mail sang;
Lance and shield both clashed and rang;
The iron and the wood, were pounded,
Shields and coats of mail resounded.
The lad heard all, but naught could see
Of those who passed so noisily;
Wonderingly he cried: 'My soul,
My lady mother twas truth she told
When she taught that devils are
The most fearsome things by far,
And, to guide me, though I cower,
To cross myself against their power.
But that sign of hers I'll disdain,
I'll ne'er cross myself; I'll deign,
Rather, to strike the mightiest
Of them with my spear, the best
I have, and these devils then
Will never trouble me again.'
Thus with himself he did argue
Before the knights came in view.
But when he saw them openly
As they rode from tree to tree,
And saw the chain-mail glittering,

And the helms, so brightly shining,
The green and the vermilion,
Glowing in the morning sun,
The gold, the silver, the azure,
Too fine and noble to ignore:
He cried: 'Ah! God, pray mercy!
These are angels that now I see.
Oh! Truly, I have greatly sinned,
With what great error I did begin,
In saying that all these were devils.
My mother's tales were no fables,
For she said that the angels were
The most beautiful things to her,
Though God most beautiful must be.
Then, God himself I think I see,
For one's so handsome, I confess,
God save me, not one of the rest
Has but the tenth of his beauty.
My mother herself said to me,
One must trust in him and adore,
Pray to him, and honour him more;
Him I'll adore, whom I see here,
And, after him, all who appear.'

LINES 155-252 THE WIDOW'S SON QUESTIONS THE KNIGHTS

THEN he threw himself to the ground,
And said the Creed, and then he found
Himself saying every prayer through
That, from his mother's lips, he knew.
The leader of the band of knights
Saw him and cried: 'Halt here! In fright,
This lad's thrown himself to the floor,

'...the chain mail glittering, And the helms,
so brightly shining'
Le Morte d'Arthur (1893), Sir Thomas Malory (15th cent) and
Ernest Rhys (1859-1946)
Internet Archive Book Images

At the sight of us; what is more,
If we advance on him together,
It seems to me uncertain whether
He might not, in his terror, die,
And thus deny me a reply
To aught of him I might demand.'
They halted there, at his command,
While he rode on towards the lad,
And sought to calm what fear he had,
Saying: 'Young man, be not afraid.'
'By the Saviour,' all undismayed,
'In whom I trust,' was his reply,
'I'm not. Are you God?' 'Faith, not I,
'Who are you then?' 'I am a knight.'
'Of such I know not, not a sight
Of one', said the youth, 'nor word,
Of any such, have I seen or heard;
Yet you are handsomer than God.
If only I, who go ill-shod,
Were made like you, and shone so bright!'
Advancing at these words, the knight
Drew near to him, and asked, swiftly:
'Have you seen here in this country,
Five knights with three maids ever?'
The youth had other things, however,
Other questions, he would advance.
He set his hand upon the lance,
Seized it, and said: 'Fair friend,
What thing is this that you extend?'
'Now am I well countered here,'
 Said the knight, 'it doth appear.
I thought, fair friend, I from you
News should have, and yet in lieu,
You seek to learn this thing of me!
Well I will tell you, tis my lance.'

Said he: 'Then tell me, do you lance
Things with it, as I with my spear?'
'No, no, my lad, you're daft, I fear!
It's used to strike a blow, fiercely.'
'Then I prefer one of these three
Spears you see in my employ,
For, when I wish, I can destroy
Any wild bird or beast, at need,
And slay them as far off, indeed,
As any crossbow bolt can do.'
'My lad, that's naught to me; but you,
Of those five knights can you tell me
If you know, where they might be?
What news of the maids can you yield?'
But the youth had grasped his shield
Tight, and in all sincerity,
Said: 'What is this, what use is he?'
'My boy,' he replied, 'this is naught;
With other subjects than I sought
You maze me, ones I did not ask!
God love me, but I saw your task
As giving me the news I needed,
Not that I truth, to you, conceded
You might wish to learn from me!
Yet since I'm drawn to you,' said he,
'I'll tell you, willingly, all the same.
This I bear is a shield by name.'
'It's called a shield?' 'Yes, in truth,
Nor must I scorn it, for tis proof,
And shows right loyal towards me,
Against all sudden blows, you see;
When aught strikes me, I yet abide;
That's the service it doth provide.'
Now those knights left in the rear
Came towards them, in full career;

To their lord they rode, at pace,
And demanded of him, in haste:
'Sire, what does this Welshman say?'
'His manners are somewhat astray,'
Said their master, 'God love me,
Naught that I ask of him has he
Replied to straight, rather, as yet,
He asks of all with which he's met
Its name, and what its use might be.'
'Sire, and you knew before, surely,
Such Welshmen as this, by nature,
Are simpler than a sheep at pasture,
This one is foolish as any sheep.
He's mad who halts here, lest to keep
Himself amused with idle play,
Or in folly waste his time away.'
'I know not, but in God's good sight,
Ere I ride onward,' cried the knight,
'I'll tell him all he wants to know,
For otherwise I shall not go.'

LINES 253-358 THE YOUTH PURSUES HIS QUESTIONS ABOUT KNIGHTHOOD

THEN he questioned him again:
'My boy, if it gives you no pain,
Tell me now of the five knights,
And if of them you've had sight,
And the maids in their company?
But by this time the lad, you see,
Had seized hold of his chain-mail,
And tugging it renewed his tale:
'Now,' he said, 'fair sire, tell me,

What you wear.' 'You know not?' said he.
'Not I.' My boy, tis my hauberk,
It weighs as heavy as ironwork.'
'Of iron, is it?' 'As you can see.'
'Well, I know naught of that,' said he,
'But, God save me, tis beautiful.
What's its worth, and is it useful?'
'That's easy lad; if you should throw
A spear at me, or fire an arrow,
You would still work me no woe.'
'God keep, then, each stag and doe
From wearing hauberks in the chase,
Fair knight, for I would never grace
My hunting with a kill again,
The hauberk would prove my bane.'
And thus the knight to him replied:
'My lad, God save you, ere I ride,
If you'd but tell me if you've seen
Those knights, and the maids, I ween.'
But he, who did small wisdom show,
Answered him: 'Were you born so?'
'Oh, no, my lad, that cannot be,
No man is born a knight you see.'
'Who then has attired you thus?'
'I'll tell you, youth so curious.'
'Well, tell me then.' 'Most willingly,
'King Arthur, he thus knighted me,
No less than five full years ago,
And gave to me the arms I show.
But tell me, now, if far or near
Are the knights that came by here,
With three maids in company;
Did they pace slowly, did they flee?
And he replied: 'Sire, look on high,
And see those woods against the sky,

That do the mountains press upon.
There lie the passes of Valbone.'
'And what of that,' said he, 'dear brother?'
'Men work the fields there for my mother,
They plough and till the fields, all day,
And if the knights have gone that way
They'd see them, and could tell you so.'
The knight replied, that he would go
Along with him, if he would lead,
To where the sowers sowed their seed.
So the youth urged on his horse
And to the fields he set his course,
And rode to where they tilled, alone,
The fields where the oats were sown.
And when their master did appear
The labourers all shook with fear.
And do you know why they did so?
Because all the knights did follow,
All armed did keep him company,
And those labourers knew if he
Had learned their nature and affairs,
He'd wish to be one, then and there,
His mother would be all distraught,
She'd want to distance him from aught
To do with knights, from being one,
Or questioning them, as he had done.
The lad now asked of the ploughmen:
'Have you seen five knights and then
Three maidens here as they passed by?
'They'll not as yet, 'was their reply,
Have finished traversing the waste.'
The lad now told the knight, in haste,
He who'd addressed him at first sight:
'Sire, they passed this way, the knights,
All five, and with the maidens too,

But tell me of this king, anew,
Who makes of men knights renowned,
And of the place where he's best found.'
'Lad,' said he, 'this to you I tell,
The king doth bide at Carduel;
And not five days ago did he
Sojourn there, it seems to me,
For I was there, and him I saw.
And if he doth not, what's more,
There are those who will know;
Not far from there doth he go,
Thus of his presence you shall hear.
But I pray you, answer me here,
By what name do they call you?'
'Sire,' said he, 'I'll tell you true,
'My name's Dear Son.' 'Dear Son, that's all?
For by some other they must call
You; yet another name.' 'Faith, sire,
They say Dear Brother.' 'Then no liar
Are you, yet if you'd speak the truth,
I'd know your true name, forsooth.'
'Then,' said the lad, 'all your desire
I'll grant: my true name is Dear Sire.'
'God save me, tis a fine name, son.
'Have you none other?' Sire, I've none;
 None that I'm called by any here.'
'God save me, wonders do I hear?
I never thought to ere come near
Such words as you send to my ear!'

LINES 359-486 HIS MOTHER TELLS HIM OF HIS FATHER

THE knight departed then at speed,
Galloped hard, being late indeed,
And long awaited by the others.
The youth now sought out his mother,
And returned to their dwelling where
She waited for him, full of care,
Sorrowing, grieving not a little.
Her joy was great at his arrival,
On seeing him she could not hide
The joy that she now felt inside,
And, as a loving mother might,
She called, as he came in sight,
A hundred times: 'Dear son, dear son,
My heart has suffered much, Dear son,
For you have been away so long.
My pain and sorrow were so strong,
That I near quit our mortal state.
Where have you been today, so late?'
'Where, lady mother? I'll tell all,
For ne'er shall lie from my lips fall,
Great joy, this day, then, did I glean,
And from a thing that I have seen.
Mother, were you not wont to say
The angels of our Lord God, pray,
Were yet so fair that in all Nature
Ne'er was made a fairer creature,
That this world could ever show?'
'Dear son, I say again, tis so.
Again, once more, in verity.'
Silence, mother! Did I not see

The fairest things that be, this day,
Pass through the Forest Waste, I say.
I thought them fairer then, by far,
Than God and all His angels are.'
She clasped him, as she had done,
And said 'God save you, dear son,
I have within great fear for you.
I do believe that you've had view
Of those angels that folk bewail
Who slay all those, without fail,
They come upon.' 'Nay, mother, nay!
Knights it is they're called, they say.'
His mother fainted at the word,
When the name of 'knight' she heard,
And when his mother had come to,
She railed as angry women do:
'Alas! Oh how I am undone!
From chivalry I hoped, dear son,
To guard you so well that never
Would you hear aught of it ever,
Nor naught of it would ever see!
A knight it is that you would be,
My fair son, if God had pleased,
If your dear father had not ceased
To raise you thus, or other friends.
No knight of yours, on this depend,
Was ever so renowned or feared
As was your father, it appeared,
Through all the Islands in the sea.
Of this you may boast, you see,
You'll not be shamed by his line,
Not by his lineage, nor mine.
From knights of old I claim descent,
The best God to this country sent;
In all the Isles, in this fair age,

None shares a nobler lineage.
But the best has been brought low;
As many another place doth show,
Vile mischance doth oft attend
On noble men who here defend
The code of honour and prowess.
Wickedness, Shame, Idleness,
Fall no lower, for they cannot,
Yet such is the good man's lot.
Your father, as you cannot know,
Was pierced through the thighs, and so
Was maimed, for life, bodily.
His great riches, land a plenty,
Which he held as a lord, dear son,
All was gone now, to perdition.
He fell into great poverty.
Impoverished, disinherited, he
Was robbed of all, in a breath,
With all the rest, upon the death
Of Uther Pendragon, the father,
He whose son is good King Arthur.
All laid waste were their lands,
And the poorer folk were banned,
And took to flight, if they could.
Your father held here field and wood,
Here within the Forest Waste;
He could not walk, but in haste
Was carried, in a litter, here
Knowing nowhere else, I fear.
And you were but a little child,
And had two brothers, thus exiled;
A child you were, un-weaned, my pet,
No more than two years old as yet.
When your brothers were full grown,
On his advice, they went alone

'And you were but a little child'
Le Morte d'Arthur (1893), Sir Thomas Malory (15th cent) and
Ernest Rhys (1859-1946)
Internet Archive Book Images

To the king's court, there indeed
To seek fine armour, and a steed.
To the King of Escavalon,
To serve with him, the first was gone;
Fought nobly, and was dubbed a knight.
The younger served, and served aright,
Beside King Ban of Gomeret.
On the same day, lest I forget,
Both were dubbed and made a knight.
And they left on the same night,
To return from their employ'
Their coming would have brought me joy,
And their father; we saw them not,
For death in combat was their lot.
Both in knightly contest died,
Great loss to me, a woe I hide.
Of the elder, sad news arose,
That the very rooks and crows,
Stole his eyes, upon that ground;
Thus was my boy, when he was found.
Grief, for his son, killed your father,
And a bitter life lived your mother,
In suffering, now that he was dead.
You were my comfort though, instead,
And all I owned; no more did bless
Me; nothing more did I possess.
God had left naught else, you see,
To bring me joy and gladden me.'

Lines 487-634 She gives him personal and spiritual advice

THE youth had listened but little
To his mother, and scarce a tittle
Had he heard. 'Bring food,' he cried,
'I know not what your words implied,
But many do go, and willingly,
To this king who, from chivalry
Makes knights; I too shall go to court.'
His mother then, although she sought
To keep him there, and have him stay,
Clothed and equipped him for the way,
Gave him a large coarse hempen shirt,
And those breeches in which are girt
Those Welshmen, where, it seems to me,
Breeches and hose are one, entirely;
And a deerskin tunic, a close fit,
And a deerskin hood to go with it.
Thus was he clothed by his mother.
Three days, he stayed, not another,
For now he would brook no delay.
Then his mother, full of dismay,
Kissed and embraced him, in tears,
Saying: 'How sad I am, my dear,
To see you go. To the royal court
Go then, and say that you sought
Him so he might grant arms to you.
I know that he would not refuse,
But would grant them you, indeed.
Yet when it comes to any deed
Of arms, how will you fare, son?

That which you have never done,
Nor hath any man shown it you;
How will you know what to do?
Ill will you do, I cannot doubt.
Ill will fare, and be put to rout.
No wonder to me, if thus you fought;
None can do what they've not been taught.
Yet failing to learn what's seen and heard,
Oft and again, proves more absurd.
Dear son, I have a lesson to teach;
So pay attention to what I preach,
And if you should my lesson retain,
Then great advantage you may gain.
Son, you will shortly be a knight,
If God so please; praise Him aright!
If you should find, or far or near,
A lady who seeks your aid, my dear,
Or a fair maiden in distress,
Who, needing aid, doth you address,
Then, should it be of her seeking,
Much honour to you it will bring.
For he who honours not woman,
Must be, in honour, but a dead man.
Maiden and lady you should serve,
If you'd be honoured as you deserve.
And if you should wish her favour,
Take care not to rouse her anger.
Do you nothing that may displease.
Who kisses a maid has won his fee;
If she deigns to grant you a kiss,
Then assume no more than this,
For my sake, seek not to linger.
But if she's a ring on her finger,
Or a purse for alms at her waist,
And through love, or of her grace,

She gives it you, tis well with me,
And you may wear the ring freely;
I give you leave to take the ring;
And the purse? Accept the thing.
Dear son, I say, twill prove a sin,
If in your lodgings, or at an inn,
You meet a man, befriend the same,
Without your asking for his name.
Fit name to person, if you can,
For by the name we know the man.
Dear son, speak you with gentlemen,
And go walk with them, and often;
A gentleman ne'er leads astray
Those who meet him on the way.
Above all else, I pray you well,
Attend at church, and go to chapel,
And pray you there to Our Lord,
That joy and honour He afford
You and, if you so continue,
To a good end will bring you.'
'What is a church, dear mother?'
'A place where we come together
To serve Him, who heaven and earth
Made, of whom all creatures had birth.'
'And a chapel?' 'That is the same,
A fine and saintly house, I name,
Filled with relics, treasures holy,
Wherein they offer up the body
Of Jesus Christ, the holy prophet,
Who, shamefully, betrayal met;
He was traduced, judged wrongfully,
And suffered mortal agony;
Died for man and woman so,
Whose souls into Hell did go,
Once they all had quit the body,

Those whom He from Hell set free.
Bound to a pillar, he was beaten,
Upon the Cross suspended then,
His head bore a crown of thorns.
So, to hear the Mass each morn,
And the Lord Christ to adore,
Attend church, as I said before.'
'Then I shall go, most willingly,
To church and to chapel, daily,'
Said the youth, 'from now on.
If tis my duty.' He'd be gone;
He would, now, no longer stay,
Takes his leave, to go his way,
Saddling his horse. She cries.
In the manner and the guise
Of a Welshman is he dressed,
Boots of hide, his very best.
But though every place he goes
He takes his three spears, and so
Would carry them along today,
His mother steals two spears away,
Since such seem too coarse to her;
And then, she would have him err
And leave all three, if she could.
His right hand held a whip, one good
For urging his fine steed along.
His mother cried that he was gone,
Done kissing him whom she adored,
Now praying for him to the Lord.
'Fair son,' she prayed, 'God grant to thee
More joy than now is left to me,
In whatever place you are.'
When the youth was not so far
As a stone's throw off, he then
Looked back at his mother again,

By the bridge, now stretched low,
And lying in a faint, as though
She were dead. But he rode on,
Whipped his steed, and was gone;
Upon its croup, he struck the horse,
It stumbled not, he set a course,
To carry him, and onward keep,
Through the forest, dark and deep.
And on he rode from morning light
Until the sun slipped out of sight,
And slept among the trees that night,
Till the day dawned clear and bright.

Lines 635-730 The youth takes the maiden's ring

At dawn, when the birds gave song,
The youth rose, mounted and along
The course he'd set he rode all day,
Till he spied a tent beside the way,
Pitched there in a lovely meadow,
Beside a stream's pleasant flow.
The tent was of a noble fashion,
One part was bright vermilion,
The other made of cloth of gold,
And it was lovely to behold;
An eagle, gilded, at its crest.
By the sun the tent was blessed
Such that all the field was lit
With the light that shone from it.
About the tent, and its surround,
The loveliest here to be found,
Had been raised two leafy bowers,
And Welsh lodges full of flowers.

The youth rode on towards the tent,
And, once there, voiced his intent:
'My Lord, this is your house, I see,
The fault were mine, assuredly,
If I entered not, to worship you.
My mother now, she told me true,
That indeed your house would be
The loveliest that I might see;
And that I must not turn aside
From any church, but go inside,
To pray to Him in whom I trust,
To our Creator; i'faith, I must
Enter, and pray that he will feed
One who asks it in great need.'
He found the tent was open wide,
And there he saw a bed inside;
With silk brocade it was o'er spread,
And sleeping there within the bed,
A maiden, all alone, saw he.
Depriving her of company,
Her handmaids had slipped away
To cull fresh flowers by the way,
And strew them all about the tent,
Its customary embellishment.
As the young man entered in,
His horse neighed, and the din
Woke the maiden from her rest,
Trembling, in fear of her guest.
And the lad, that simple youth,
Said: 'I greet you maid, as proof
Of what my mother taught to me.
My mother said, where'er I be,
That I should greet every maiden
In every place I came upon them.'
The maiden, trembling with fear

'*Flee before my lover spies You here*'
Le Morte d'Arthur (1893), Sir Thomas Malory (15th cent) and
Ernest Rhys (1859-1946)
Internet Archive Book Images

Of this fool, in his strange gear,
Thought she herself truly shown
To be the fool, caught thus, alone.
'Boy,' she said, 'avert your eyes,
Flee before my lover spies
You here.' 'By my life', said he,
'I'll kiss you first, whoever sees,
As my dear mother told me to.'
'I'll ne'er receive a kiss from you,'
Cried the maid, 'against my will.
Flee lest he comes, for he will kill
You if he does, thus tis your death.'
The lad was strong and, in a breath,
He had clutched her in his embrace,
Not knowing how to kiss with grace,
Such that she lay beneath him there,
While she struggled, in mock despair,
To free herself whene'er she could,
Though her efforts did little good,
For he kissed her, willing or no,
Twenty times, so the tale doth go,
Planting kiss after kiss upon her,
Till he spied a ring on her finger,
An emerald, and the stone did shine.
'Now,' said he, 'that mother of mine
Said I might take it from your finger,
But beyond a kiss might do no other.
Your ring, however, I shall take.'
'You'll ne'er have it, make no mistake,'
Said the maid, 'and that I know,
Unless, with force, you rob me so.'
The lad now took her by the hand,
Grasped her finger, as he'd planned,
Slipped from it the emerald stone,
And placed the ring upon his own,

Saying: 'My maid, tis a fine deed!
Now paid in full shall I go, indeed;
And much finer kisses are yours
Than the chambermaids' indoors,
That at my mother's house, I faced,
For yours have not their bitter taste.'
She wept, and said to the lad: 'No, no,
Take not the ring there from me, so,
For he will take your life from you,
And I shall suffer for it too.'

LINES 731-830 THE MAIDEN TELLS ALL TO THE KNIGHT, HER LOVER

THOUGH she promised he would pay,
The lad heard nothing she did say;
And, since he'd yet had naught to eat,
Half-starved, was dying on his feet.
He looked about him then and spied
A bottle of wine, and at its side
A silver goblet, and next he saw,
On a sheaf of rushes what's more,
A fresh towel, all new and white.
He lifted it and, a welcome sight,
Found three venison pasties there;
All overjoyed was he at the fare!
Since his hunger was eating him,
He broke ope the one before him,
Tackling the whole thing greedily,
Then filled the silver cup and freely;
For it troubled him not to keep
Drinking often, and drinking deep.
He said: 'My maid, there is no way

I could eat all these three today,
Come and eat then, for they are fine;
If you have yours, and I have mine,
One of them will be left here still.'
But, as if bereft, she wept her fill;
Though he begged her and implored
Not a word would she say more;
The more indeed she wrung her hands
And wept the harder, at his demands.
The youth meanwhile ate on and on,
And drank the wine till it was gone.
He covered the food that remained,
And took his leave of her again,
Commending her to God, although
His parting word, as he turned to go,
Was: 'God save you, my sweet friend,
For God's sake be not troubled again,
If I carry away your ring,
For I'll repay you for the thing
Before I die, thus I promise you.
Now I must take my leave of you.'
But she wept and said that never
Would she commend him to God, ever,
Since through him she'd have to bear
More shame, a greater load of care,
Than any wretch had borne before.
Nor, while she lived, she was sure,
Would she see from him any aid,
And thus by him was she betrayed.
She was left weeping at this same;
But now from the woods there came,
Not long after, the knight her lover,
Who was dismayed to discover
Hoof prints where the horse had been,
And his lover weeping there, I ween.

He spoke out: 'Demoiselle, I fear
Given the signs that I see here,
That some knight has been with you.'
'There was none, sire, I swear, tis true,
For a Welsh lad only did appear,
A greedy wretch, the oaf was here,
Who has drunk all your good wine,
All that there was, and found it fine,
And ate some of your pasties three.'
'Then, why do you cry, my sweet?
If he had eaten all, why grieve,
I would yet have given him leave.'
'But there is more, sire,' she said,
'My ring he took before he fled,
Stole it, and carried, it away.
I wish that I were dead this day
Rather than that he had the ring.'
Now this to him distress did bring,
And he was wounded to the heart.
'T'faith,' he said, 'a villain's part!
Now let him have it, since it's gone,
Yet I think a further deed he's done.
Hide it not, had he more from you?'
'Sire,' she said, 'he kissed me too.'
'Kissed you?' 'Truly, and yet still,
He kissed me all against my will.'
'Rather you were pleased to kiss
And in no manner did you resist,'
Said he, now filled with jealousy.
'Think you I know you not, indeed?
I know you thus, and all too well,
I'm not so one-eyed, not so blind
That your falseness I cannot find.
You've entered on an evil way,
Along a path of ill you'll stray,

No fodder shall your palfrey eat,
Till my revenge is had, complete.
And if your horse doth shed a shoe,
I'll not re-shoe him e'er for you.
If he dies, you'll follow on foot,
And ne'er renew your clothing, but
Instead of keeping the clothes you wear,
Follow on foot, stripped naked, bare
To the world, till I have his head;
I'll take no other payment instead.'

LINES 831-928 THE YOUTH, ON HIS WAY TO COURT, MEETS THE RED KNIGHT

THE knight then sat him down to eat,
While the youth rode, till he did meet
A charcoal-burner who was, that day,
Driving his mule, along the way.
'Good fellow, you, behind the mule,
The shortest way now, to Carduel,
Please tell to me,' said the youth.
'I wish to see King Arthur, in truth,
Who makes knights, or so they say.'
'My lad,' he answered, 'go that way,
For he has a castle beside the sea.
You will find, my friend, 'said he,
If to that castle you go, that glad,
King Arthur is, and yet also sad.'
'Now, tell me, for I would know
Why the king feels joy and sorrow?'
'I'll tell you that, at once,' said he.
'He's delighted with his victory
Over King Rion of the Isles;

Regarding Rion's loss, he smiles
At defeating him with all his men,
Yet he is angry with his friends,
Who to their castles have departed,
Leaving the king broken-hearted;
For they prefer to sojourn there,
Nor doth he know now how they fare.'
The youth gave not a penny-nail
For the charcoal-burner's tale,
Except he entered on the road,
He was shown, this he followed
Till he found a castle by the sea,
Well-sited, strong, and fair to see.
And he saw issue from the gate
A knight, bearing, as if in state,
A cup of gold in his right hand.
His lance and shield in his left hand
He held, and grasped the reins tight,
And only the cup held in his right.
His armour glittered in the sun,
And it was all bright vermilion.
The youth saw his weapons too,
Which were also fresh and new,
And they pleased him, so he said
'I'll ask these of the king, instead.
If he grants them, then twill be fine,
Curse him who seeks another kind!'
He hastened on to Arthur's court,
Come late to the castle he sought,
Such that he found the red knight near.
And the knight, seeing him appear,
Detained him there, upon the way:
'Where are you off to, lad, I say?'
'I wish,' said he, to reach the court,
And ask the king for arms, I thought

To ask for yours.' 'My lad, tis well,
Go swiftly now, and this king tell
Of my words, go tell the cowardly
Fellow if he'll not hold from me
His lands, then he must surrender,
Or send some knight, his defender,
Against me now, for they are mine.
Let him give credence to this sign,
I've carried his golden cup away
From which he drinks, this very day,
And every drop that it contains.'
The king, indeed, might prove fain
To send another champion,
For not a word retained this one.
The youth departed for the court
Where the king, whom he sought,
And all his knights were at table.
The hall he entered; as 'twere a stable,
Twas on the level, and paved inside,
And it was long as it was wide.
And King Arthur there held court,
At the table's head, lost in thought.
The knights around were chattering,
And laughing, jesting, bantering,
Except the king who, silent, mused.
The youth arrived, but now confused
Knew not which man he should greet
As king, his ignorance complete,
Till Yvonet, we understand,
Came to him, carving-knife in hand.
'Fellow,' said the lad, 'on my life,
You who hold the carving-knife
Tell me now, which is the king?'
Yvonet, courteous in everything,
Told him. 'Friend, you see him there.'

So to the king the youth repaired,
And greeted him, as best he knew.
The king, in silence, mused anew,
The lad spoke, thinking he'd not heard,
Once more; the king said not a word.
'I'faith,' the youth said, 'day or night,
This king has never dubbed a knight.
How? When a fellow can't be heard,
Nor can he make him speak a word!'

Lines 929-1060 Kay, the Seneschal, scorns the youth

THE youth now turned his horse's head
Prepared to ride away instead.
But so close to the king did go,
Proving the fool, in acting so,
That in a trice, without a lie,
The king's bonnet was knocked awry,
And fell upon the table, dead.
The king now raised his head,
And turned it towards the lad,
Forgetting what thoughts he had,
Saying: 'Welcome, sir, if I
Was silent, and gave no reply,
Then take it not amiss, you see
I could not; my worst enemy,
The greatest there could ever be,
Who hates and most troubles me,
Has laid a claim to all my lands
And says that he, you understand,
Shall have them all, will I or no;
The Red Knight, for they call him so,
Of Quinqueroi, is his true name.

The Queen also heard his claim,
For she was sitting by me here,
To comfort and to bring good cheer
To those wounded knights you see.
He would scarce have angered me,
Whatever he had said, but he
Seized my cup, most recklessly,
And raised it high in such a way
That all the wine it bore did spray
Over the queen; such was the shame
And coarseness of his act, aflame
With her indignation and distress,
To her room she has fled, no less,
And there she is troubled unto death,
Nor is it thought, by God's breath,
That she shall escape it, utterly.'
The youth gave not a fig, not he,
For a single word the king had said,
Nor cared the queen was well-nigh dead,
From all the shame, nor for her plight.
'Lord King,' said he, 'make me a knight,
For I would be off, upon my way.'
Clear and bright the gaze, that day,
Of our young savage; from his eyes
None who saw him thought him wise,
But everyone who viewed him there
Thought him noble, in this affair.
'Friend, dismount then,' said the king,
'This squire shall see to everything
Your steed requires, and willingly
Fulfil your wishes, graciously.
You'll be dubbed, by God, I own,
To my honour and your renown.'
To all of this, the youth replied:
'That knight did not dismount, outside,

He whom I'd yet hold to account,
And yet you wish me to dismount!
No, on my life, I'll not descend,
Do all, and let me thither wend.'
'Ah!' said the king, 'dear boy', said he,
'I shall do so most willingly,
To your renown and my honour.'
'By the faith I owe my Creator,
My Lord the King,' the lad replied,
I'll not be a knight by your side,
If the Red Knight I cannot be.
Grant me the arms then that he
Wore, when I greeted him outside,
Bearing your golden cup, in pride.'
The Seneschal, whose wounds still bled,
Was angered by the words he said,
And cried: 'My friend, you say aright,
Go and take them from this knight,
You met outside, for they are yours.
You were no fool to state your cause,
By coming here, and claim them thus.'
'Kay, by God, 'have mercy on us,
You jeer too readily,' said the king,
You should show no scorn for him.
Tis the worst vice in a nobleman.
If he's but raw, yet an honest man
He seems, and though he comes to court
As one we see who's been ill-taught,
By a wretched master, yet he may
Prove wise and noble some fine day.
It's wrong to jeer at another
And promise what you fail to offer.
A gentleman to another ought
Never to make promise of aught
That he cannot or will not give,

Lest resentment choose to live
In one, who would have been his friend
But for the promise he did extend,
And who thinks twill be fulfilled.
From this, indeed, we see tis still
Better to grant not, in the main,
Than let a man hope on, in vain.
And, whoe'er the truth would tell,
That man deceives himself full well,
Who makes a promise, then refuses;
For his friend's heart thus he loses.'
So did the king admonish Kay.
Meanwhile the lad turned away,
And came upon a lovely maid.
He greeted her, and was repaid;
She greeted him, and then she smiled,
And said this to him, as she smiled:
'Young man, if you live long enough,
I believe, in my heart, you'll prove
That in all the world there's not,
Neither known, nor e'er begot,
A better knight than you will be.
I think so, it seems so to me.'
And she'd not smiled this fair maid,
For a good six years. All I've conveyed
To you she said, she said out loud,
So all heard. And Sir Kay, the proud,
Sprang at her, riled by what he'd heard,
Struck her a blow, without a word,
With his palm, on her tender face,
Such that she fell flat, in that place.
When he had slapped her he sought
To return to his place, and caught
The Fool by the fire; and with his foot,
He kicked him into the ash and soot,

In his hot anger, while on his way,
Because the Fool was wont to say:
'That girl won't laugh, nor smile shall she,
Until one day she'll chance to see,
A man who over chivalry
Shall hold utter sovereignty.'

LINES 1061-1199 THE YOUTH KILLS THE RED KNIGHT

THE fool did cry and she did weep;
The youth upon his way did keep,
Despite a lack of good advice,
And found the Red Knight in a trice.
Meanwhile Yvonet who knew
The byways, and sought what's new,
And relayed it all at court,
To his companions, in short,
Ran through an orchard by the hall,
Slipped through a door in the wall,
And came out on the road aright,
Where before him our new knight
Looked for chivalry and adventure.
And now the young man, at a venture,
Flew at him, whose arms he sought,
And who, awaiting him, had brought
The golden cup, and set it down
On a stone there, of mottled brown.
When the youth had ridden near,
So each one could the other hear,
The youth cried: 'Lay down your arms,
You'll no more with them wreak harm;
Do as King Arthur now commands!'
Of him the Red Knight made demand:

'My lad, doth no one dare appear,
To maintain the king's right here?
If none will do so, hide it not.'
'What the devil? A joke, or what,
Is this among you knights, that you
Have failed your armour to remove?
Off with the lot, tis my command.'
'Fellow,' said he, ''twas my demand
If any will come and, for their king,
Fight with me; declare the thing!'
'Sir knight, now doff armour and all,
Or I the armour from you shall haul,
I'll suffer you to wear it no more,
Know well I'll fight you, for sure,
If you should make me speak again.'
At that, the knight, in angry vein,
Seized, in both his hands, his lance,
And gave the lad a blow that glanced
Across the shoulders, and such was it,
That though with the blunt end he hit,
He made the lad bend low, the force
Bowing him o'er the neck of his horse.
And the youth was angry indeed
When he felt his shoulders bleed
From the strength of that blow.
Best he could, at the eye of his foe,
The lad let his sharp javelin fly;
The knight saw no more nor heard;
It flew through the eye to his brain.
The man's heart failed, with the pain,
And down the neck, about the nape,
The lad saw brains and blood escape.
The knight collapsed to the ground.
The lad dismounted then, and found
The lance, and put it to one side;

The helm was next, but it defied
All his efforts to drag it free.
Then he attempted, eagerly,
To win the sword, but knew not how,
Could not unsheathe it anyhow,
Yet pulled and tugged at it awhile.
Now Yvonet began to smile,
Watching the lad toil and bend:
'What is it now,' said he, 'my friend
That you do?' 'I know not, indeed,
I thought the king, for this deed,
Would grant his red armour to me.
But I will have to chop, I see,
The corpse to little pieces fine,
If I would make his armour mine.
Tis strapped so tightly, and more,
Both behind, and here before,
That to my eye it seems all one,
So intricately is it done.'
'Be not troubled by anything,'
Said Yvonet, 'if you wish the thing,
I know how all this may be had.'
'Then do it, swiftly,' said the lad,
'Hand them to me without delay.'
So Yvonet started, straight away,
To strip the corpse from head to toe.
Left it nor mail-leggings nor hose,
Helm on its head, nor other armour.
But the lad would not, however,
Leave off the clothes he wore that day,
For aught that Yvonet could say,
And take the quilted tunic, fine,
Of woven silk, as soft as mine,
That when alive, the knight had worn,
Beneath his mail, all quite untorn.

He could not make the lad divest
Himself of his boots, nor all the rest.
'The devil' he cried 'what jest is this?
Exchange my clothes, if that's your gist,
That mother made the other day,
For this knight's sad attire, I say?
Swap my fine thick hempen shirt
For his which is but thin and curt?
Would you have me leave this off,
My coat the sharp rain bounces off,
For his, that every drop will soak?
Cursed be he, who e'en his cloak
Will exchange who, now or later,
Accepts ill gear when his is better!'
Tis very hard to teach a fool;
Naught but the armour would that mule
Accept; all pleas they were in vain.
Yvonet laced up the mail amain,
And in the hauberk saw him clad,
The best that any ever had,
And set the helmet on his head,
Till twas well-set, then he wed
The sheath to the belt tightly,
Yet so his sword swung loosely;
Set his foot in the knight's stirrup,
Steadied the horse, and he was up.
He'd ne'er seen a stirrup before,
Nor of spurs knew he much more,
Only a stick or a willow-switch.
Yvonet brought the shield which
He gave to him, and then the lance.
Then as Yvonet sought to prance
Back again, the lad said: 'Friend,
Take my mount, you can depend
On him; he's fine; and now indeed

Of that good fellow I've no need,
And take this cup back to the king,
And so to him my greetings bring;
And then that maiden you must seek
Whom Sir Kay struck on the cheek,
And say, ere I die, if I but can,
I'll take the measure of the man,
And as her revenge twill rate.'

LINES 1200-1300 THE FOOL PROPHESIES REVENGE ON KAY: THE KING GRIEVES

THE squire said that he would straight
Return the cup, and would convey
His message to her, on the way.
Repassing the door in the wall,
Yvonet joined the lords in the hall,
And returned the cup to the king.
He said to him: 'Sire, a joyful thing;
I bring you your gold cup this day,
The cup your knight returns, I say,
The knight who has but lately gone.'
'What knight is this you speak of, son?'
The king said, who with shame and ire
Wrestled yet. 'In God's name, sire,'
Said Yvonet, 'the young man who
Not long ago was dubbed by you.'
'Of that young Welshman then you speak,
Who did the arms and armour seek,
That knight's armour, painted red,
Of him who's done his best to wed
Me to ignominy and shame?'
'Sire, in truth, the very same.'

'And my cup, how was it won?
Did that recreant knight, my son,
Return it of his own accord?'
'No twas dearly sold, my Lord,
For the youth struck him dead.'
'How come, my sweet friend?' he said.
'Sire, I know not, and yet I saw,
The Red Knight, indeed, make war
Upon him, strike him with his lance,
But then the youth he did advance,
Hurled a spear that pierced the eye,
Drove out blood and brains, say I;
So to the ground the knight did fall,
And he lies there stone dead withal.'
Said Arthur to the Seneschal:
'Ah, Kay, you've worked ill in this hall!
From your scornful tongue there fell
Idle words that, indeed, may well
Have driven that young man away,
Who does me good service this day.'
'Sire,' said Yvonet to the king,
'Upon my life, a message I bring
To the handmaid of the queen
The girl that Kay struck, I mean,
Out of jealousy, hate and spite;
That he, if he lives, will fight
To avenge her; tis his desire.'
The Fool, who sat beside the fire,
Heard his words, leapt to his feet,
Sought the king, his joy complete,
Danced and skipped, ready to sing,
And said: 'God save me, my king,
Now your adventures are begun.
Many a long and perilous one,
You will find, shall come to you;

And I make you this pledge too,
Kay can be certain sure that he
Will regret those hands and feet,
And that foolish, hateful tongue,
For ere a fortnight shall be done,
This young knight, he will repay
The blow from his foot, this day,
And that buffet he gave the maid,
At high cost too shall be repaid,
And he'll be well requited so,
For twixt the neck and the elbow,
Sir Kay's right arm he will break;
For half a year, for our two sakes,
May he carry that arm in a sling!
Like death he'll not escape the thing.'
His words grieved Kay so deeply,
That for a while he was completely
Overcome, so, by rage and spite,
In front of all, he almost might
Have ensured the Fool's decease.
Yet since the king it would displease,
He restrained his malice that day.
And the king said: 'Ah, Sir Kay,
You've angered me, and I am sad!
If you and I had trained the lad,
And taught him how to use a lance,
Behind his shield how to advance,
What precautions he should take,
Doubtless a fine knight he'd make;
But he knows neither good nor bad.
When it comes to arms, the lad
Knows scarcely how to draw, indeed,
The sword he bears, in time of need.
And sitting there, upon that horse,
He'll meet some other lad, of course,

Who will not hesitate to fight,
And win his steed from our poor knight.
He'll die at once, or wounds enjoy;
He's such a raw and simple boy,
Defenceless, he will be dismayed.
Soon his quietus he'll have made!'
Thus the king spoke his regret,
Grieving for the youth, and yet
There was naught that he could do'
Thus a fresh silence did ensue.

Lines 1301-1415 The youth reaches Gournemant's castle

THROUGH the forest spurred the youth
Without a moment's rest, in truth,
Until he reached the level plain
And found a river that did drain,
Being a crossbow shot and more
In width, the whole land; to its shore,
And its deep bed, all waters ran.
Towards the river, he now began
To make his way across a field,
But to the water would not yield
His mount; twas dark and deep below,
And swifter than the Loire its flow.
He kept instead along the bank,
Across from the rugged flank
Of a tall cliff, on the other shore
Against which the current bore.
Upon this cliff, sloping down
Toward the sea was set a town,
Castellated, rich and strong,

'*Towards the river, he now began*'
Adapted from Le Morte d'Arthur (1893), Sir Thomas Malory
(15th cent) and Ernest Rhys (1859-1946)
Internet Archive Book Images

And where the river, running on,
Met the bay, leftwards he turned,
Sight of the castle towers he earned,
Which looked to him as if, some morn,
From out the clifftop they'd been born.
Within the castle, at its heart,
He saw a mighty keep, apart.
A barbican before it lay,
Facing out towards the bay;
Its walls did confront the sea;
On it the waves beat equally.
The four corners of the wall,
Of solid stone built withal,
Four fine lower turrets graced;
Strong towers opportunely placed.
The castle was well-situated,
Trim within and strongly-gated.
Before the gatehouse, moreover,
A tall bridge spanned the water,
Sandstone, limestone there allied,
Such that the bridge was fortified
With crenellations left and right;
At its centre, there rose to sight
A tower; and a drawbridge lay
Before it, built to serve by day
As a true bridge, as was right,
But as a barrier at night.
Towards the bridge, the youth now rode,
A gentleman upon it strode,
Who an ermine robe did wear;
He, indeed, was waiting there.
He held a short staff in his hand,
To add an air, you'll understand;
And after him came squires two,
Lightly-dressed, but smartly too.

'Its walls did confront the sea;
On it the waves beat equally.'
Adapted from Le Morte d'Arthur (1893), Sir Thomas Malory
(15th cent) and Ernest Rhys (1859-1946)
Internet Archive Book Images

He waited for this newcomer,
Who the words that his mother
Had said to him, still retained,
For he bowed, and then explained:
'My mother taught me so to do.'
'God bless you, my brother, too.'
Said the lord, who saw in truth
The lad was raw still, and uncouth,
'Where then do you come from, brother?'
'Why, from the court of King Arthur.'
'What did you there?' 'Why, there the king
Made me a knight, and may that bring
Him luck.' 'A knight? God bless me so,
I'd not have thought that, now, you know,
He'd be concerned with such a thing,
For I'd have thought perchance the king
Had other thoughts than making knights.
But tell me brother, and say aright,
Who gave you your arms and armour?'
'The king, indeed, good King Arthur.'
'He gave them, how?' And he retold
His story; twould strike you as old;
Who tells his tale, and then again,
He proves a bore, for tis in vain;
No tale demands a second telling.
The gentlemen progressed to asking
How the youth employed his steed.
'I make him charge about, indeed,
O'er hill and dale, as I used to do
With that horse I had, that I knew
At the house my Mother doth tend.'
'And of your arms and armour, friend,
You'll tell me what you know of them?'
'Why, how to clad myself and doff them,
The way the squire himself taught me,

Who disarmed the body, carefully,
Of that one I slew, the fallen knight.
And the arms themselves feel light,
Indeed they weary me not at all.'
'By God, I delight in that, withal,'
Said the gentleman, 'it pleases me.
Now say, if it is no grief to thee;
What need of yours has led you here?'
'Sire, from my mother I did hear,
That I should meet with gentlemen,
And she gave me her counsel then,
That I should act as they advise,
For he who acts so all men prize.'
The gentleman replied: 'Dear brother,
Blessings indeed upon your mother,
For she truly counselled you well.
But you desire…no more, do tell?
'Yes.' 'Then, what?' This, and no more,
That you lodge me here, I do implore.'
'Most willingly,' said the gentleman,
'If to me a favour you'll grant,
From which great benefit you'll see.'
'That is?' the youth said. 'That from me
You take good counsel, and your mother.'
I'faith,' said he, 'and I shall, moreover.'
'Then, dismount!' and he descended.

LINES 1416-1534 GOURNEMANT TEACHES THE YOUTH HOW TO BEAR ARMS

ONE squire held, as his lord intended,
The guest's horse, while the other
Helped divest him of his armour,

Leaving him in the clothes he had,
And hide boots, but roughly clad
In his deerskin tunic, an ill fit,
His mother's gift, for she made it.
The spurs, then, of sharpened steel
The lad had brought, on his heels
The lord strapped, and did mount
On the horse, on his own account;
Hung at his side the shield of red,
Then grasped the lance tight, and said:
'My friend, of arms now shall you learn,
Watch carefully, and thus discern
How one ought to wield the lance,
And check a horse, and advance.'
And then he unfurled the banner,
And showed the lad the manner
In which a shield should be held;
To show his art he felt compelled,
Settling it before him, a little,
Till the steed's neck felt the metal,
And placed the lance in its rest.
He spurred the steed, of the best,
Worth a hundred marks, for none
Went more willingly, and not one
Showed greater spirit in the field.
The lord knew much of the shield,
Of horse and lance; great skill he had,
For he had learned when but a lad.
Our knight was pleased at the skill
The gentleman could show at will.
When he had performed his drill
Before the youth, who took his fill
Of gazing, and had pleased the eye,
He returned, his lance raised high,
To the youth, did of him enquire:

'My friend, tell me, do you desire
To learn to wield the shield and lance,
And how to check steeds and advance?'
Then the youth said, right away,
That rather than live another day,
Or gain a wealth of land to sow,
How to act thus he would know.'
'What a man knows not he can learn;
If he takes care to attend, in turn,
He'll be an expert, my fair friend.
On but three things doth all depend,
Three things required in every trade:
The effort, practice, heart displayed.
And since you have practised naught,
Nor gazed at others, nor been taught,
Knowing not how to do the same,
In that there is no shame or blame.'
Then the expert made him mount,
And he gave such good account
With lance and shield, it was as though
He'd all his life spent his time so,
At tournaments and in the wars,
And ridden seeking, without pause,
Through every land, for adventure;
Because it came to him by nature.
And when Nature yields the art,
And it involves the whole heart,
Nothing then too grievous proves;
If heart in line with nature moves.
With those in play, he did so well,
The lord was pleased, and could tell
In his heart, that if the youth
Had all his life done so, in truth,
Drilled and performed, to the letter,
He might well have done no better.

When the youth ceased his turn,
To the lord's feet he did return,
And with his lance raised, too,
Just as he'd seen the master do:
And said: 'Sire, have I done well?
If I so wished it, can you tell,
If I would master, then, this thing?
I've ne'er laid eyes on anything
That I have coveted so greatly.
I wish I knew as much, truly,
As you of arms and armour know.'
'Friend, set your heart upon it so,'
Said the lord, 'and you will learn;
About that I have small concern.'
The lord mounted three times more,
Three times showed him, as before,
All he knew that might be shown,
Having him mount thrice, on his own,
Till the youth had been well fed.
As the lad reined in, at last, he said:
'If a knight you chose to encounter
What would you do, if thereafter
He struck you?' 'I'd strike him back.'
'And if your lance broke in attack?'
'I could do no more, in the lists
Than have at him with my two fists.'
'My friend, do not do so, I pray.'
'What should I do then? 'Have away
At him with your sword; fence instead.'
He took the lance and planted it dead,
Upright, in the ground before his feet,
Thinking the youth should complete
His training now, in arms and armour,
So that he might defend his honour
With the sword, if that were needed,

Or attack if ground were conceded.
In his hand he took the sword, now,
And said: 'My friend, this is how
You must defend if you're attacked.'
'God save me,' the lad said, 'as to that,
None knows as much of that as I,
For on targets, like bolsters, have I
Worked, at my mother's house until
I was often weary, and am so, still.'
'Then, into the castle go, dear brother,
For as to lodgings there's none other;
Whoe'er objects, this night you'll see
Saint Julian's hospitality.'

LINES 1535-1592 THE YOUTH DECIDES TO RETURN TO SEE HIS MOTHER

AND in they went, then, side by side,
And the youth, when they were inside,
Declared: 'Sire, my mother taught me
That I should ne'er keep company
With any man, or be with the same
For long, if I knew not his name.
This she thought and taught me so.
Thus your name, sire, I would know.'
'Dear friend, tis a matter of report;
My name? Gornemant of Gohort.'
Thus the castle the two now entered,
Proceeding, hands clasped together,
And were met at the entrance stair,
By a squire, all unprompted, there,
Who bore a cloak and, though twas short,
Wrapped the lad in what he'd brought,

So that the youth might take no chill
After his practice, and thus fall ill.
A rich dwelling, both fine and grand,
This lord had; fair servants to hand,
Who hastened his dinner to prepare,
Of good, well-cooked, plenteous fare.
They washed their hands and, that complete,
Sat down at the table to eat.
The lord placed the lad at his side,
And to the same dish they applied
Themselves. I'll speak no further
Of what the meal comprised, other
Than to say they had enough to drink,
And more than enough to eat I think;
I'd not serve you a meal from fable.
When they rose, and left the table,
The lord, who was most courteous,
Said twould be advantageous
If he could stay a month or two,
Or a whole year, if he chose to;
He would host him willingly,
So that he might learn more fully
Such skills, that is if he agreed,
Which he could use, when in need.
The youth replied: 'Sire, tis unclear
Whether I'm far from or quite near
The house where my mother dwells.
But I pray that the Lord God tells
Me the way, grants me this boon:
That there, where I saw her swoon,
I'll see her standing, when I arrive.
For I know not if she's alive,
Or dead, and yet I must confess
That when I left her, the distress
May well have caused the swoon, and so

The state she's in I need to know,
I cannot stay here, I must follow
The road from here, at dawn tomorrow.'
The lord on finding even prayer
Was of scant use, fell silent there.
And they retired thence to bed,
All being ready; no more was said.

LINES 1593-1696 GORNEMANT'S ADVICE ON CHIVALRY, INCLUDING TACITURNITY

THE lord rose from his bed at dawn,
And went to find the lad, that morn,
Still lying in his bed, and brought
The lad a welcome gift, he thought;
A shirt, and breeches of fine linen,
A coat of violet silk, woven
In India, and hose dyed red
With brazilwood dye, and said,
Thinking that twas time his guest
Had risen and was fully dressed:
'Friend, if you place full trust in me,
Dress now in these clothes you see.'
The lad replied: 'If you did desire,
You might advise otherwise, sire;
Those my mother made; they please,
And are they not worth more than these?
Yet you'd wish me in these to dress!'
'My boy, I swear, on my head no less,'
Said the lord, 'these clothes are better.
That you'd obey me to the letter,
You promised me, my young friend,
Before we hence our path did wend.'

'And so I shall,' declared the lad,
'Most willingly, and shall be glad
To oppose you in naught you say.'
He dressed in them, without delay
Discarding those from his mother.
And the lord bent and laced a spur
To the lad's right foot, for, you see,
The custom was, in chivalry,
That whoever did make a knight,
Should lace the spur on his right.
And there were squires there also
Who each enough of arms did know
That thus a hand they might afford.
The nobleman took up the sword,
And kissed and embraced the lad,
And he declared that now he had
Conferred on him, with that sword,
The highest order of Our Lord,
Which is the order of chivalry,
That needs be free of villainy.
And said: 'Dear brother, keep in mind
That if yourself you should find
In combat with another knight,
I say, and pray of you, outright:
That if you have the upper hand,
Such that he can no longer stand
Against you, not even to defend,
But rather begs to make an end,
Cries 'Mercy!' then kill him not.
And may these words not be forgot:
Talk not too much, nor too freely,
For none can speak for long ere he
Says something oft, along the way,
That smacks of villainy. They say,
The wise, to themselves within:

'Who speaks too much commits a sin.'
So I, dear brother, forbid you to
Talk too much, and I beg of you,
If some girl or woman you find,
Or a maiden or a lady, mind,
Who seems in any way distressed,
Counsel her, aid her, do your best,
If you can pluck counsel's flower,
And to do so is in your power.
Another thing I must explain,
And hold you it ne'er in disdain,
For ne'er disdained should it be:
Go to church, and willingly,
Pray to Him who made us all,
His mercy on your soul befall,
That in this mortal life, of man,
He guards you as a Christian.'
And the lad said, to the lord:
'Bless you fair sire, tis assured,
For, by all the saints in Rome,
My mother said the same at home.'
'From now on, my dear brother,
Ne'er say that from your mother
You learned aught,' said the lord,
'I blame you not, and I've ignored
Your mention of her, since you came,
But from now on supress the same,
For you'll be taken for a fool,
The object of men's ridicule;
From this day forward, if you please.
Let this bad habit of yours cease.'
'Dear sire, what then should I say?'
'To this true gentleman you may
Attribute all, who laced your spur,
Say that he taught you, and not her.'

The youth said that, from now on,
He promised ne'er to sing that song,
While he lived, not a single word
From out his lips would be heard;
For all he'd taught him was fine.
The lord then chose to make the sign
Of the cross, hand raised on high:
'God save you, then, fair sir! For I
See that twould trouble you to stay.
God go with you, and guide your way.'

Lines 1697-1771 The Castle of Beaurepaire

THE new-made knight now departed
The castle, eager to be started
On his return to his good mother,
Alive and well, he hoped to find her.
Passing through the forest again,
Which, better than the level plain,
He'd known since a child was he,
He rode along till he did see
A castle, strong and well-sited.
Before the walls naught he sighted
But ocean, water, and wasteland.
Towards the castle there at hand
He rode, till he reached the gate,
But feared then to trust his weight,
To a bridge that might not bear
Him, such that ill he might fare.
Yet our knight the bridge he mounted,
Without encumbrance, accounted
For his passage and, free of shame,
To the portal our knight then came,

'*Towards the castle there at hand He rode*'
Le Morte d'Arthur (1893), Sir Thomas Malory (15th cent) and
Ernest Rhys (1859-1946)
Internet Archive Book Images

Which he found under key and lock,
And twas not gently he did knock,
Nor did he call out soft and low.
He knocked so loud, down below,
That to the window there did sail,
Of the hall, a maiden, thin and pale.
She cried: 'Who are you that call?'
The youth on looking up, saw all,
And said: 'Fair friend, a knight and true,
Who doth humbly beg of you
That I might enter, and as a knight,
Find lodging here for the night.'
'Tis well,' she said, 'sire, if tis your
Wish; you'll thank us not, I'm sure.
Yet nonetheless we'll treat our guest
As well as we can; and do our best.'
And then the fair maid withdrew.
While he, who waited there anew,
Fearing he would be left outside,
Knocked again, and loudly cried.
Four men-at-arms swiftly came,
Who held great axes, and the same
Had each a fine sword at his side,
And they the portal opened wide,
And beckoned: 'Sire, enter then!'
They'd all have proved fine men,
Handsome indeed, except that they
Were suffering, and in sorry way,
(Twas enough to make one weep)
From hunger and from lack of sleep.
And if, outside, the youth had found
The earth a wasteland, barren ground,
The inside did naught to amend it;
For every place there he did visit,
He found the streets all desolate,

And saw the houses ruined straight,
Scarce man or woman to be seen.
There were two churches, that had been
Abbeys once, within the town,
In one, frightened nuns he found,
In the other, monks most wary.
He found that neither sanctuary,
Was handsome or in good repair,
The walls, indeed, were cracked and bare
And roofless too were the towers;
The buildings naked at all hours
To the elements, night and day.
No mill there ground its corn, I say,
None baked bread for house or hall,
Naught there was found, no food at all,
Nor was there aught a man might buy
You'd give a denier for, nor I.
Thus he found the town laid waste;
And not a crust of bread to taste,
Or wine to drink, no cider or ale.

LINES 1772-1942 THE MAIDEN BLANCHEFLOR

THEY led him, the soldiers weak and pale,
To a slate-roofed palace, without harm,
Then helped him dismount, and disarm.
And soon a squire came down the stair
And met him, as he was waiting there,
Who bore in his arms a cloak, all grey;
He placed it round his neck, and away,
To stable his horse, then ran another,
Though his steed he would discover
Had naught to eat, nor oats nor hay,

Nor any wheat; they'd none that day.
The squires went before him there,
And thus the knight mounted the stair,
To enter the hall; twas fine and grand.
There stood a maid; on either hand
Two gentlemen, their hair not quite
Turned from grey to snowy white,
Of sound health, for all their years;
Had they not borne woes and fears,
They'd have been most handsome men.
The maid approached the young man then,
Finer she than a young goshawk,
A falcon or a sparrow-hawk,
In elegance and gracefulness.
Her mantle and her black silk dress
Were starred with gold; no wear
Showed on the ermine border there;
And her cloak's collar did display
A wealth of sable, black and grey,
Cut not too long, nor yet too wide;
To expose the neck, or yet to hide.
And if I have e'er homage paid
To some beauty God has made,
To a woman's body or her face,
I'm pleased my words to retrace,
Once more; and yet I tell no lie.
Head unadorned, her hair, say I,
Was such that any there to see
Might have thought, if such could be,
That it was spun from finest gold,
It shone so bright and fair, all told.
Her forehead, pale, smooth, set high,
Seemed as if it twas sculpted by
An artist, by some master's hand,
In marble, wood or ivory planned.

'*The maid approached the young man then,*
Finer she than a young goshawk'
Le Morte d'Arthur (1893), Sir Thomas Malory (15th cent) and
Ernest Rhys (1859-1946)
Internet Archive Book Images

With fine eyebrows widely spaced,
The eyes, well-set within her face,
Glinted blue-grey, smiling, clear.
Her nose straight, neat, did appear;
And the pure crimson over white
Of her cheeks was lovelier quite
Than scarlet blazoned upon silver.
The Lord created her a wonder,
To steal away the heart of man;
Nor had He e'er, since time began,
Made her equal, nor has He later.
As soon as the knight beheld her,
He greeted her, and she replied,
As did the knights at either side.
And as the maid demurely led
Him by the hand, she sweetly said:
'Dear brother, you tonight will find
Your lodgings here are of a kind
Unfit for any gentleman.
Yet if those present now began
To speak here of our misery,
You might think that it might be
They spoke of it with ill-intent,
As if on your departure bent.
But, if it be your wish that is,
Find lodging here, such as it is;
God send you better, tomorrow.'
Hand in hand, he then did follow
Into a room, its ceiling vaulted,
Long and wide, where they halted,
Then sat them down upon a bed
With a samite cover o'er-spread.
They sat together, side by side;
Then there made their way inside,
In fours, fives and sixes, knights

Who also sat and, lips sealed tight,
Gazed at the youth who sat beside
The maid, as if he were tongue-tied;
For he held himself from speaking,
Within that lord's advice repeating,
Who too much talking did deplore;
And thus twas not too long before
The knights began a conversation.
'Lord,' each said, in consternation,
'Do you suppose this knight is mute?
Twould be a pity, for who'd refute
No fairer knight was born of woman.
He looks so well beside our maiden,
And she looks well beside the knight.
Would they were not so dumb a sight,
For she's so lovely, and he so fair,
No knight or maiden would, I swear,
Be matched so beautifully together.
For it seems, of one and the other,
That God made each for the other,
So that the two might be together.'
And all those who sat around them
Their conversation was about them.
And the lady sat there hoping
That the youth might utter something,
Until to her it seemed quite clear
No word from him would appear,
If she were not first to speak to him.
So, graciously, she said to him:
'Whence do you come, sir, this day?'
'Fair maid,' he said, 'last night I lay
At the castle of a noble lord,
And goodly lodgings did he afford;
Five towers, all strong, it had got,
One was tall, and the others not.

I know how to describe the same,
Yet I know not that castle's name.
Though the name of the lord I sought,
And twas Gournemant of Gohort.'
'Ah! Dear friend,' the maiden said,
'You speak aright, upon that head,
And you speak most courteously.
May God who is our King bless thee,
Twas "noble lord" I think I heard.
You'll never say a truer word,
By Saint Richier, noble he is;
And I can well attest to this.
For, know that I am that lord's niece,
Though I have not seen him apiece;
And truly, since you left that place
You'll not have come face to face
With a finer gentleman, I'll swear.
He'll have lodged you gladly there
As only he knows how to do,
For he is noble and gracious too,
Powerful, well-served, and rich,
While all I have is five crusts which
An uncle of mine, most glorious,
One most saintly and religious,
Has sent me for supper tonight,
And a flask of wine, a sour white.
Of food indeed I have no more
But for one fine roebuck I saw
My lad slay with a bow this day.'
Then she told her servants to lay
The tables, and they were thus laid,
And swiftly all the supper made.
They sat but little over their meal,
For with it swiftly they did deal,
And after eating left the keep,

Except for those who were to sleep
Who'd been awake the night before,
The rest departing, the youth saw,
Who were to form the guard that night.
Fifty, the men-at-arms and knights,
Who comprised this castle guard,
While the other men worked hard
To honour and to please their guest.
With white sheets and with the best
Of coverlets, they prepared his bed,
And set a pillow at its head.
Thus every ease, every delight
A bed might provide at night,
Had the youth; yes, everything,
Except the joy a maid might bring,
If to desire the lad had bowed,
Or a lady, if twas allowed.
But, of all that, the lad knew naught,
So I say there was scarcely aught
To keep him from falling asleep
Since he had no watch to keep.

LINES 1943-2072 BLANCHEFLOR SEEKS THE YOUTH'S HELP

BUT the maiden, most distressed,
Within her chamber could not rest.
He slept at ease, while she thought;
For her protection she had naught,
Against the siege set to assail her.
She tossed and turned there in fever,
Much troubled, and as pale as milk.
Then, a short cloak of scarlet silk,
She draped about her chemise,

And ventured forth, if you please,
All brave and resolute in action,
Yet not for any idle reason,
Rather she thought she would go
To her guest and speak, although
She'd tell but a part of her affairs.
She rose from her bed and dared
To issue forth from her chamber,
So fearful, that her every member
Trembled, body bathed in sweat.
Tearfully, from the room she set
Out for the chamber where he slept
And there she loudly sighed and wept;
Yet dared do little more than weep.
She knelt by him as he did sleep,
And her tears fell at such a pace
They wet the surface of his face.
She cried so hard that he awoke,
Wondering, as the drops did soak
The sheets and run from his face,
And felt himself in her embrace,
Who knelt before him, in the night,
Clasped his neck, and held him tight.
He showed enough plain courtesy
As to take her in his arms, for he
Drew her towards himself and cried:
'Fair one, why are you at my side?
What is it then you desire of me?'
'Ah! Gentle knight, have mercy!
By God, I pray you, and his Son,
Think me not the shameful one
For coming here to you like this.
Though I am almost naked, tis
Not that I intend some folly,
To work you some ill or villainy,

But there's none other on this earth
So full of grief, devoid of mirth,
That I outdo them not in sorrow.
And I shall feel the same tomorrow,
For nothing now can bring me ease,
Each day proves ill, so sad to me,
That I'll not see another night,
Except it seems for this one night,
Nor other day except the morrow,
But kill myself, and die in sorrow.
Of three hundred knights and ten,
There now remain but fifty men
By whom this castle is manned.
Ten score and sixty he unmanned,
The cruel knight, who seized all,
Engygeron, who is Seneschal
To Clamadeu of the Isles, he
Killed them, or forced captivity
On them. I grieve for those he led
To prison, as I do for the dead,
For I know he'll kill them too,
None can escape his purview.
For me, so many men must die,
Tis right that I should grieve and cry.
Besieged have we been here
A winter and a summer clear,
By Engygeron; he moves not,
But adds to the force he's got,
While ours has dwindled away;
Our supplies, as you see today,
Such that what remains on hand
Will scarce feed one single man.
And we are brought to such a pass,
That tomorrow, if God, alas,
Does naught for us, tis at an end;

The town we can no more defend.
And I must be surrendered too.
Rather than that alive he mew
Me, I will kill myself and, dead,
Will care not if my corpse is wed
To Clamadeu, who would possess
Me, yet shall have me not unless
I am emptied of soul and life.
For in my casket I keep a knife,
A weapon made of finest steel;
Its point my poor heart shall feel.
And now indeed I've told you all,
And I'll return, ere aught befall,
And leave you here to take your rest.'
Honour might accrue to her guest
If he but dared, the new-made knight;
She had not come to him that night,
And with her tears thus wet his face,
Except with sole intent to place
Him under some deep obligation,
To defend the town, take station
Before their ranks, if he dare stand,
And fight for her, and for her land.
And he answered her: 'Dear friend,
Be of good cheer, till night's end.
Comfort yourself, do not weep
Come closer to me, and so keep;
Brush those tears from your eyes.
If God wills it, He shall devise
A better morrow than you say.
Beside me in this bed now lay
Your head, tis wide enough for two.
Don't leave me till the day is new.'
She said: 'If you wish it so.' At this,
He turned and gave the maid a kiss,

And held the maid in his embrace.
Over their bodies he did place,
Gently, and tenderly, the cover;
And she suffered him to kiss her,
I think it caused her no annoy.
And there they lay, girl and boy,
Beside each other, all that night,
Lip to lip, till the morning light.
So the night brought her solace,
For lip to lip, arms interlaced,
The two both slept till it was day.
At dawn the maiden slipped away
And thus returned to her room;
Without help, we must assume,
She found her clothes and dressed,
While all slept, as did her guest.

LINES 2073-2157 THE YOUTH GOES TO FIGHT ENGYGERON

YET those who'd watched all night
Once they caught the morning light,
Roused all those who were asleep,
Stirred all who their beds did keep,
And thus they all rose with the day.
And then the maid, without delay,
To her young knight did repair,
And said to him, quite debonair:
'Sire, may God give you good day!
I know you must no longer stay,
Nor must you linger in this place,
And to no end our presence grace;
You must go, but I'll grieve not,
Twould be discourteous, our lot

Is not to sorrow at such a thing,
For we have not done anything
In point of comfort or of ease.
And now I pray that, if God please,
He'll help you on, to lodgings fine,
With more bread, and salt, and wine,
Than you have found here this day.'
He said: 'Fair maid, and yet today,
I shall no other lodgings seek,
Until this land, of yours I speak,
I have restored to you, if I can.
If I should find that evil man
Twill weigh on me if he remain,
For I'll not have you grieve again.
But if I death upon him wreak,
Then your affection I will seek
As my reward, it shall be mine;
All other prizes I'll decline.'
And she replied, with courtesy:
'Sire, the prize you ask of me
Is a poor thing and despised.
Yet if I refused, I am apprised
That you might think it pride;
Thus you shall not be denied.
Yet tell me not, by God above,
That I am to become your love,
Through such an act of loyalty
That you go forth to die for me;
For that would be too great a shame'
Your age, you strength, your fame,
Are not yet such, you may be sure,
That you could e'er contend in war
With one so hardened in the fight,
Nor meet and conquer such a knight.'
'Well that will soon be seen,' said he,

For I go to fight him, he'll meet me;
I'll not forgo this, nor brook delay.'
She pleaded with him in such a way
As to deter him, though twas her wish.
It often happens we serve the dish
Yet mask the contents carefully,
When someone suitable we see,
Whom we'd send upon a mission,
To better rouse the man's ambition.
This did she, and most skilfully,
Reproaching him so forcefully,
While rousing it within his heart.
He said to bring his arms, and start
To arm him, and they did so straight.
And went and oped the outer gate,
And once armed they set him high
Upon a steed they had, twas nigh
Him, saddled, amidst the square.
And there was not a person there
Who was not troubled, all did say:
'Sire, God bring you aid, this day,
And may misfortune now befall
Engygeron, the Seneschal,
Who has laid this country waste,'
As down their cheeks the tears raced.
To the gate they led him and, when
They saw him leave the castle, then
Called out, as one, to ward off loss:
'Fair sire, now may the True Cross,
On which God gave his Son to suffer,
From mortal peril guard you ever,
From every mishap and from prison,
And bring you to, in calmer season,
A place where you may rest at ease,
That delights you, and doth please.'
Thus for him the people prayed.

LINES 2158-2329 ENGYGERON IS DEFEATED AND SENT TO ARTHUR'S COURT

THE soldiers saw him, there arrayed,
And pointed out Engygeron,
Before his tent, his chain-mail on,
His hose of chain-mail, laced ready,
His men rejoicing already,
Who thought that they must easily
Seize the castle and the country,
Thinking too all would be done,
The castle rendered, ere the sun
Set, or there appeared someone
To fight their lord, one to one.
When Engygeron saw him there,
He armed himself for the affair,
Rode towards him at full speed,
On his strong and sturdy steed,
And cried: 'Fellow, who sent you here?
Why? To what end do you appear?
Do you come seeking peace or war?'
'And you, what is your presence for?
Tell me, first, why you seek this land?
Why do brave knights die at your hand?
Why do you lay these fields to waste?'
And now Engygeron proudly faced
The bold youth, saying, haughtily:
'This very day the keep must be
Emptied, and the town surrendered,
Which has been too long defended.
And my master shall have the maid.'
'Cursed be the day that thus conveyed

Such words, and he who speaks them now!
Soon, when I challenge you, I vow
You'll swiftly renounce that claim.'
'What idle talk you serve, and lame,
By Saint Peter,' cried Engygeron,
'Tis often that the simpleton,
Who's free of guilt, must pay the price.'
The youth who'd stirred once or twice
Couched his lance, and without delay
To close contest each made his way;
Swiftly each man made his advance.
A trenchant blade and ashen lance
Had each, and sharpened at the tip;
The horses reared, with foaming lip;
Fuelling hatred, with every breath,
Each man sought the other's death.
So furious now is their encounter,
The shields and the lances splinter,
Each forcing the other to bow low.
But once more to the fight they go,
Meeting together with clenched jaws,
More savagely than two wild boars,
Striking to pierce the other's shield,
And force the fine chain-mail to yield,
Whene'er their steeds bear them close.
With the rage and speed each shows,
And their strength as each advances,
The bits and pieces of their lances
That remain fly through the air.
Engygeron was unseated there,
He alone, and wounded beside,
Such that his left arm and his side,
Caused to him most grievous pain.
But the youth dismounted again;
No use now for his steed he found,

From his horse, leapt to the ground,
Drew his sword, and then set to.
I know no more I can tell to you
Of what happened to each knight,
The blows each landed in the fight,
But long did they fierce battle wage,
And many a blow was dealt in rage.
Until Engygeron fell back.
So fierce then was the lad's attack,
That the Seneschal cried mercy,
But the youth said he would see
No mercy now, not now or ever.
But then he recalled, however,
The gentleman who'd said, at will,
He should not, in conscience, kill
Any knight whom he'd conquered,
Who cried mercy, and surrendered.
'Dear friend,' the Seneschal did cry,
'Be not so cruel, as to deny
Your mercy, have mercy on me!
I swear to you most willingly
That I am worsted in this fight
And you prove the better knight;
Not that it would be believed
By any man who had perceived
Us both, or knew of us, before
That you, with but the arms you bore
Could bring me so close to death.'
But if I bear, with my own breath,
Witness that you conquered me,
My men before my tent shall see
Me swear the very same to you,
And more honour will accrue
To you than any knight before.
And think, if there is some lord

Who's shown his favour to you,
And had no guerdon for it too,
Well then, send me, and I shall go,
On your behalf and he shall know
How by arms you did conquer,
And render myself his prisoner,
To do with me as he sees fit.'
'Cursed he who seeks greater forfeit!
Know you where I'll send you then?'
Said the youth, 'to the castle, and when
You find the maid who is my friend
Tell her, that till your life doth end,
You will ne'er seek to do her harm,
Nor cause her any other alarm,
But shall be wholly at her mercy.'
'Kill me now, at once,' said he,
'For she will kill me then, dear sire,
And nothing more doth she desire
Than my death and sore disgrace.
For when her own father did face
Death, I was there, and I have so
Angered her, all her knights, my foe,
I have captured or killed this year.
You grant me ill prison, I fear,
If to her prison I am sent.
You could show no worse intent.
But if you have no other friend,
Nor mistress, then do you send
Me to some better place, where
They'll hate me not for this affair,
For she indeed will have my head.'
The youth said he might go instead,
To the lord's castle, the very same,
And there must tell that lord his name.
In all the world lived not a mason

Who could devise the fashion
Of that place, as that lord had done.
He praised the water that did run
Beside it, bridge, towers and keep,
The walls, the cliffs, high and steep,
Till the knight feared he was fated
To go to where he was most hated
And find himself imprisoned there.
'At such a place, ill would I fare,
Dear sire, if there you'd send me.
God save me, on paths of misery
You'd set me, and in ill hands;
For in the wars upon these lands
I did slay there his own brother.
I would have you slay me rather,
If tis to him you would send me.
Better you kill me now, than he.'
'T'faith,' the youth said, 'then go
As prisoner to King Arthur, so
Greet the king, as sent by me,
Speak, on my behalf, directly,
Say you would the maiden see,
Whom Kay the Seneschal, sourly,
Did strike; she did on me confer
A smile; render yourself to her.
And tell the maid that not for aught
Shall I return yet to that court
Where King Arthur reigns whate'er
May happen, so I promised her,
Until I have avenged the blow.'
And he replied that he would go,
And perform that service truly.
Then, to the town, the youth, whom he
Had been defeated by, did ride,
While Engygeron turned and, on his side,

Rode to the court; while his banner
Was struck; thus the siege was over,
And all departed, the dark and fair.

Lines 2330-2431 Clamadeu plans to attack Beaurepaire

THOSE of the castle soon were there
To welcome those who now returned.
But were troubled when they learned
That he'd not killed the foe, instead
The conqueror had spared the head,
Nor had he rendered him to them.
Yet they still welcomed him again,
With joy, and helped him to disarm,
Sure now that he was free from harm;
Saying: 'Why did you choose, Sire,
Though the man's death we desire,
Not to take Engygeron's head?
'My lords,' said he, 'i'faith, I said
To myself that twould not be well;
And as he slew a host of your kin,
I could not guarantee him within;
You'd have slain him, despite me.
Little honour had it brought me
Had I denied mercy to a man
When his life was in my hand.
Know you the mercy I confer?
He'll be King Arthur's prisoner,
If he acts now as we did agree.'
Then the maid came, joyfully,
And greeted him, and then she led
Him to her room, where, she said,
He might rest and take his ease.

And she was happy not to cease
From hugging and kissing there;
Instead of eating, drinking, their
Fare was hugging, kissing, play;
Many a sweet word did they say.
But Clamadeu, who folly sought,
Launched an attack, for he thought
The castle was defenceless yet;
But then upon the road he met
A squire who was full of sorrow,
And the tale did quickly follow
Of Engygeron, his seneschal.
'God help us, ill doth us befall,'
Cried the squire who, in despair,
Tore, with both hands, at his hair.
And Clamadeu answered: 'How?
And the squire: 'I'faith, but now
Your seneschal was beaten here,
And, is pledged, it doth appear,
To take himself to Arthur's court.'
'Who has done this? Come, report;
How has this mishap come to be?
Whence comes this knight, that he
Could force so fine a knight's surrender,
The true and brave a prisoner render?'
'Fair Sire, indeed,' answered he,
'I know not who the knight might be,
But I do know I saw one there,
Who issued forth from Beaurepaire
In crimson armour, with these eyes.'
'Well then, what would you advise?'
Cried Clamadeu, half mad with rage.
'What, sire? Return,' replied the page,
'For I perceive, if you advance,
You'll soon be led a merry dance.'

At this, an old knight came in view
Who had trained young Clamadeu,
Whose hair indeed was almost white
'Young man,' he said, 'it is not right,
Better, wiser counsel than yours
He needs if he's to fight his wars.
If he heeded you, a fool he'd prove.
My advice is this: a forward move.'
The squire said: 'Sire, would you know
How you might deceive them, so
As to take the castle and the knight?
I'll tell you, and I'll tell it right,
And tis but the simplest affair.
Within the walls of Beaurepaire,
They have naught to drink or eat,
Their garrison's weak, incomplete,
While all our men are fit and strong,
No thirst or hunger's here among,
And we could endure the longer
If they dared, we being stronger,
To issue forth and seek to fight.
We'll send a troop of twenty knights,
To offer them such, before the gate.
The young knight who yet dallies late
With Blancheflor his fair lover,
Would prove his chivalry to her,
But he'll be utterly mistaken,
For thus he'll be killed or taken,
And little help to him will be
Their weak enfeebled infantry.
Our twenty will attempt naught there
But to draw them from their lair,
While we advance, by this dale,
And creep upon them, our detail
May then attack them from behind.'

'T'faith, cried Clamadeu, 'I find
Tis fine, all that you have to tell.
We have here our elite, as well
Five hundred knights fully armed,
A thousand soldiers all unharmed,
Our enemy are as good as dead.'

LINES 2432-2521 CLAMADEU'S ATTACK FAILS

So Clamadeu, as the lad had said,
Sent twenty knights toward the gate,
Who, in the wind, deployed straight
Each his standard, his brave banner,
Blazoned in heraldic manner.
When they were seen from inside
Then the gates were opened wide
Because the youth wished it so,
Who issued forth, ahead did go,
To meet the advancing knights.
Bold and fierce now, in a fight,
The lad attacked the whole set,
Nor did he seem, to those he met,
Merely an apprentice still;
He managed his arms with skill,
Skewering many with his lance,
Piercing many, in his advance,
In neck or chest, breaking bone,
An arm here, there a collar-bone,
Crippled one, downed another,
Captured him, and to a brother
Knight, in need, he gave the mount;
Till they saw a host, made count
Of a good five hundred knights,

Ascending the dale, to the fight;
A thousand soldiers there beside,
Sweeping onwards, like the tide,
Towards the open gate; but then
The enemy see their fallen men,
The pile of injured, and the dead,
And thus unsettled, charge instead
In wild disorder, at the gate,
While those before the castle wait,
In serried ranks, all patiently,
And so receive them steadfastly.
Yet they were weak indeed and few,
While the enemy forces grew
As fresh men followed in the rear;
So, yielding, as they drew near,
Those at the gate made their retreat.
Archers above the gate did greet
The foe, shooting them en masse
As they fought ardently to pass,
Till a small group forced their way
Beyond the wall and sought to stay.
Then those above, within the town,
Dropped a great portcullis down
Upon the enemy, there below,
Crushing and slaughtering the foe,
With the mighty force of its fall.
And Clamadeu could scarce recall,
A sight that brought him greater woe,
Than witnessing that mortal blow.
His people dead, himself denied,
It forced a halt there in mid-stride,
While fresh assault, begun in haste,
Would merely prove a futile waste.
That lord, again, did him advise,
Who had at first the plan revised.

Saying: 'Tis no great wonder, sire,
Among noblemen, if plans misfire.
For good and ill fall, as we know,
On us as God wills; joy or woe.
You've lost some men, yet they say
Every saint has their feast day.
Upon you did the tempest fall,
Your men fought ill, while theirs stand tall,
But they will lose yet, to my mind.
Pluck out my eyes, leave me blind,
If they're alive in three days' time.
The castle and the tower are prime
For taking, at your mercy they
Must surely be, if you but stay
Here today, and then tomorrow.
Then victory will surely follow,
The castle will be in your hands;
She who scorned all your demands,
Will pray God you'll deign to take her.'
His pavilion was raised, moreover,
And those the lords had brought,
While the others lodging sought,
As best they could, for the night.
Within the castle all those knights
Who were captive were disarmed,
But not imprisoned there or harmed.
Having pledged most solemnly,
As knights sworn to fidelity,
That each man was a prisoner still,
And he would seek to do no ill.
Thus the arrangements within.

Lines 2522-2622 Fresh supplies reach Beaurepaire

THAT same day a mighty wind
Drove a vessel ashore, complete
With a welcome load of wheat
And many other victuals too.
As God willed it, good as new
Came that cargo from the sea.
And when the vessel they did see
Those within sent to enquire
Whom it bore, and their desire.
And they said: Merchants are we,
Who seek out trade, upon the sea.
We've salted-bacon, bread and wine,
And cattle to sell you, and swine,
If such things might meet your need.
And they replied: 'Blessed, indeed,
Is God, who made the gale to blow
That drove your ship to windward so,
For you are all most welcome here!'
Let all your cargo now appear,
Discharge your load, for we will buy;
You may sell all, the price as high
As you wish; and we'll encumber
You with ingots, beyond number,
Bars of silver, and bars of gold,
Too many e'en to count, all told.
And as for all the meat and wine
A cart or two we'd have you line
With the like, more if you need.'
Both had what they sought indeed,
Those who bought and those who sold.

They started emptying the hold,
And had the cargo sent ahead,
That those within might now be fed.
When those in the castle did see
The cargo carried from the sea,
You may believe, all was delight,
And as soon as e'er they might
They hastened to prepare a meal.
A longer siege, for woe or weal,
Must Clamadeu, stalled outside,
Impose, for all the folk inside
Had beef and pork and salt bacon,
In plenty; bread, wine, venison.
No longer idle, the cooks toiled,
The lads lit fires, the cooks boiled,
Toasted, roasted, stewed and fried.
Our knight could linger long beside
His lover, wholly at his ease,
Hug and kiss her as he pleased.
Each one brought the other joy.
The hall once more did all employ,
Echoing with delight again,
Delight with all the load of grain,
And meat, and wine, they'd desired;
The cooks worked as if inspired;
Whose need was greatest there, a seat
Now took, at table, and did eat.
They rose, others took their place.
But Clamadeu did grieve apace,
At the news he now had heard
Of what fortune had conferred
On those within; some said retreat,
They'd not starve now they could eat;
There was no battle to be fought,
They'd besieged the town for naught.

But Clamadeu, incensed, irate,
Now sent a message to the gate,
Ignoring counsel or advice.
He sought the red knight to entice,
Saying that, till noon tomorrow,
He might find him, to his sorrow
If he sought him, and if he dared.
When the maiden heard, she flared
With anger, she was sore aggrieved
By this challenge he'd received;
Yet, in answer to his foe's demand,
Word was sent, at his command,
That he would fight him, as he sought.
Deep her distress then, at the thought,
Yet he'd have fought on the morrow,
However great the maiden's sorrow;
He would not have stayed, for aught.
Now one and all, within the court,
Begged him not to meet a knight
Who'd ne'er been conquered in a fight
By any he had met before.
'My Lords, were you to say no more
That would be well,' said the youth,
'For I'll be stayed by none, in truth
By no man who's upon this earth.'
Of speech then there was a dearth,
For, of those present, none dared speak;
They retired, their rest to seek,
Till the dawn when the sun arose.
Yet they still grieved; Lord knows,
They'd failed to find an argument
That might have altered his intent.

LINES 2623-2717 CLAMADEU IS DEFEATED AND SENT TO ARTHUR'S COURT

His friend begged the youth that night
Not to go forth next day, and fight
Again, but stay with her, in peace,
For they cared not a penny-piece
For Clamadeu and all his men.
Yet all in vain her pleading then,
And that was wonderfully strange,
For wide her tenderness did range,
From kisses soft to kisses sweet,
And each word with a kiss did meet,
So sweet, so soft, she set Love's key,
Consolingly, yet coaxingly,
Within the lock that is the heart.
And yet she failed, despite her art,
In persuading him to yield
And keep from the battlefield,
Rather his arms he did demand.
The squires under his command
Bringing arms and armour, quickly
As they could, armed him swiftly,
Though one and all there did grieve,
And he, one and all, as he did leave,
Did commend to the King of kings,
A fine Norwegian steed mounting,
Which a squire to him had brought,
For then the battlefield he sought,
Unhesitatingly, he went,
Leaving them there to their lament.
When Clamadeu saw the man appear

Who must fight him, and draw near,
He thought, within, most foolishly
That he would very quickly free
The lad, before him, from his saddle.
The ground it was fine and level,
And there were only those two there,
Clamadeu's men removed elsewhere,
He having sent his troops away.
Each man now his lance did lay,
Fronting the saddle, on its rest,
And, without challenge or arrest,
Each on the other did advance.
An iron tip to his ashen lance,
A pliant weapon, had each man,
Strong indeed, and the horses ran
Full tilt; the men, at every breath,
Showing their hatred unto death;
They met, and their bucklers cracked,
Their lances shattered in attack,
And both were borne to the ground;
Yet both leapt up and, with a bound,
Knight again encountered knight,
And each maintained an equal fight
For a long while, with his sword.
A full description I might afford
To you, should I seek so to do,
But, as for that, why trouble you,
When one word's as good as twenty;
For Clamadeu, begged for mercy
Despite himself, when all was done.
He pledged all to him who'd won,
As his seneschal had, if only he
Might not (twas the Seneschal's plea),
Be sent to those at Beaurepaire,
And, at best, imprisoned there;

Nor, for all the wealth of Rome,
Be sent to Gornemant's home,
That fine keep; a place unfitting.
And yet, if it came to promising
To go and seek out King Arthur
As his prisoner, he would rather;
And give the girl his message, she
Whom Kay had struck at, viciously,
Causing her such great distress:
That he'd avenge Kay's churlishness,
If God would aid him so to do.
The youth extracted this pledge too,
That on the morrow, at first light,
All those he held, each captive knight,
Clamadeu must straight set free;
And, while he was alive, that he
Must drive off any foe whatever
That might besiege the castle ever,
Nor must he, nor e'er his men,
Trouble the demoiselle again.
Thus Clamadeu departed and,
When he'd regained his own land,
Commanded all those imprisoned
Be now released from every prison,
And so the captives all went free;
According to the pledge, that he
Had made, so his will was done.
And then the prisoners, every one,
Carrying all they might possess,
Left at once, free from distress,
For none now detained them there.

LINES 2718-2879 ENGYGERON AND CLAMADEU ARRIVE AT ARTHUR'S COURT

UPON another path, did fare
Clamadeu, who went alone.
It was then a custom, known,
I find it in the text writ fair,
That a knight made prisoner
Must go where'er he was sent,
Attired as from the field he went,
The field in which he'd been undone;
For not one garment he had on
Could he remove, or don the new.
Thus, in such guise, did he pursue
His seneschal, Engygeron,
Straight toward Dinasdaron,
Where King Arthur held his court.
At Beaurepaire, I can report,
All was joy when those returned
Who had, as prisoners, they learned
Suffered long and grievously.
All the hall was filled with glee,
And the lodgings of the knights,
And the churches, with delight,
Rang out their bells, every one;
And nor was there a monk or nun
Failed to give their thanks to God.
Through the streets, gaily shod,
Danced the people, one and all,
Great the noise within the hall;
Ended was all siege and war.
But Engygeron, gone before,

And Clamadeu, journeyed on.
Three nights the latter resting on
Some bed where the first did sleep.
Thus at his heels doth closely keep,
Till near Dinasdaron in Wales,
Where Arthur at his court regales
A mighty gathering. Here, we see,
Clamadeu, enter presently,
Alone, in armour as is right;
Engygeron perceives the knight,
Who has arrived the day before,
Given his message, and said more,
Then retired, with more to tell;
And is retained at court, as well,
In Arthur's entourage and council.
He saw his master's armour still
Stained with blood, dyed all red,
But knew him yet and loudly said:
'My lords, tis wondrous to see!
The lad with the red armour, he
Has sent him here, I think it true;
The one now approaching you,
I'm sure the lad has conquered;
And tis why he's blood-covered.
Yet I, despite the blood, can tell
Tis he himself beneath, full well.
I am his man; and he my master;
Clamadeu of the Isles, no better
A knight in all of Rome's Empire
A knight who all men doth inspire,
I thought drew breath; yet on a reef
The best of men may come to grief.'
Such words did speak Engygeron
While Clamadeu came striding on.
Each now ran the other to greet

And in the courtyard they did meet.
Twas Pentecost, and there the queen
Sat beside King Arthur, I ween,
At the head of the dais, among
Many a count and king, a throng
Indeed, of queens and countesses.
And this was after all the Masses
Being said, from church the men
And women had returned again.
And Kay strolled about the hall,
All uncloaked, as it did befall,
In his right hand was his baton,
His velvet cap he there had on,
Crowning his wealth of blond hair,
No finer knight alive was there,
The hair close-plaited in a braid;
Yet the handsomeness displayed,
Was offset by his wicked tongue.
His coat indeed was fit to be sung
In song, a deep rich crimson dyed.
With a handsome belt it was tied,
Its buckle and trim were of gold,
As I well recall, for thus tis told;
And the book I have bears witness.
All made a path for his progress,
As he strode, there, about the hall.
His wicked tongue twas, above all,
They feared, and so they all made way.
Not wise those folk, I would say,
Who fear not jibes, grave or in jest,
With malice openly expressed.
Those who stood about the hall,
So feared his taunts, one and all
Avoided any speech with him.
And now he chose to stir a limb,

Go to where Arthur sat, and say:
'If you wish, fair Sire, you may
Dine now, or whene'er you please.'
'Kay,' said the king, 'leave me in peace.
By these eyes set in my head,
I'd not eat at so grand a feast, I said,
Before the full court, in plenary,
Until some fresh news came to me.'
While he spoke of what he sought,
Clamadeu, approached the court;
Both holding himself a prisoner,
And in the armour he must wear,
And said: 'May God save and bless,
The finest king, as all do confess,
The most noble and most generous
Here now, on this earth, among us,
As witnessed by each and every one,
Knowing the great deeds he has done!'
So hear me now, fair Sire,' said he.
'And listen to the message, that he
Who conquered me, bade me bring;
Yet it pains me to say the thing,
Even though I dare admit no less.
Like it or not, I must confess
Myself your prisoner, by his command.
Yet if any here were to demand
If I know that knight's true name,
I must say: I know not that same,
But this much can to you be said,
That all his armour is crimson red,
And twas you that sent him, verily.'
'Friend, then, so may God aid me,
Tell me, in truth,' replied the king
If he is well, despite everything,
Healthy, sound in limb, and free.

'Yes he is, and most certainly,'
Said Clamadeu, 'fair Sire, I own
He's the bravest knight I've known,
And proved the most skilful as well,
And he's commanded me to tell
The maiden who smiled at him,
And was struck by Kay, on whim,
Landing a vile blow on her face,
That he'll avenge that disgrace,
If God will but grant his consent.'
When the Fool heard his intent,
He leapt for joy, and cried aloud:
'May God bless me, Sire, I vowed
She'd have payment for that blow,
Twill prove no lie, I told you so,
For Kay will bear a broken arm,
Against that he'll find no charm,
Twixt neck and shoulder, I fear.'
Kay, who his prophecy did hear,
Took it all with a pinch of salt;
And that he mounted no assault
On the Fool, showed no cowardice;
But shame, and the king, did this.
For the king now shook his head,
'Ah, Kay, it grieves me much!' he said,
That the lad's not here, with me.
That tongue of yours and its folly
Banished him, to my great regret.'

LINES 2880-2969 THE YOUTH SETS OUT TO RETURN TO HIS MOTHER

To the castle, and so claim it ever,
Assuredly, and, moreover, he said,
He'd do the same if she were dead.
The journey was his main concern,
Though he'd promised he'd return,
His friend he was bent on leaving
She anguished, now, and grieving,
And all the other folk cast down.
When he issued from the town
So great was the sad procession,
Twas like the Day of Ascension.
Forth all the monks had poured,
As if twas the day of our Lord;
With them the silk cope prevailed;
And all the nuns, who were veiled.
Each man and woman cried: 'Lord,
'You, that the exiled have restored,
Returned us to our dwelling-place,
It is no wonder you see each face
Wet with tears, to see you leave.
So deeply now do we all grieve,
No deeper could our sorrow be.
But he replied: 'Weep not for me;
Naught here should make you cry.
For think you not tis well that I
Go seek my mother as I should,
Whom I left there in the wild wood,
The one they call the Forest Waste?
Whether she lives or not, in haste

Shall I return, nor fail in aught.
If she lives, she shall be brought
To you and she shall take the veil,
Or, if she be dead, I shall prevail
On you to pray that she'll reside
In Abraham's bosom, there abide;
And so each year mark her death-day.
Good monks, and pious ladies, say
What is there to grieve you here?
I shall enrich you, have no fear,
If God so wills it that I return.'
Then the monks and nuns did turn
To their sanctuaries, and the rest
Departed, while, with lance in rest,
Armed, as he came, he went his way.

Lines 2970-3068 The Castle of the Fisher King

And on he journeyed all that day;
Yet encountered nothing human,
Neither Christian man nor woman,
Who might point him on his road;
Nor ceased to pray, as on he rode,
To the Glorious King, his Father,
That He'd lead him to his mother.
And he continued, praying still,
Until, descending from a hill,
He saw a river there below;
Swift and deep the current's flow.
He gazed at it, but saw no ford.
'Ah! Dear God, Almighty Lord,
Could I but reach the other side,
If she's alive and well,' he cried,

'My house is in the neighbourhood,
Between the water and the wood'
Adapted from Le Morte d'Arthur (1893), Sir Thomas Malory
(15th cent) and Ernest Rhys (1859-1946)
Internet Archive Book Images

'Then, indeed, I'd find my mother.'
So he rode on, along the river,
Until a cliff he neared apace;
There the water touched its face
Such that he could ne'er pass by.
And then a small boat met his eye,
Floating swiftly down the stream.
And, therein, two men sat, abeam.
While one man steered, by design,
The other fished with rod and line.
He stopped to wait, for he thought
That, as they flew on, they ought
To pass him closely, by and by;
Yet they stopped, as they flew by.
Then he spied the anchor gleam,
And they anchored in mid-stream.
And he who with line and hook,
Was seen to fish, the bait he took,
And then attached a little fellow,
Scarcely larger than a minnow,
To his hook. Not knowing where
To cross, he greeted then the pair,
Called aloud, and asked of them:
'Can you advise me, gentlemen;
Is there a bridge to the other side?'
And he who fished, he then replied:
'T'faith, dear brother, there is none,
And then, for twenty miles, not one
Vessel, I do believe, afloat
Larger than is this, our boat,
And this will only carry five.
On horseback none pass alive;
There's no ferry, bridge or ford.'
'Tell me then, by God our Lord,
Where I may find a place to stay.'

And he replied: 'You'll need, I'd say,
That and more, if I judge aright;
Tis I will lodge you for the night.
Ride up through that gorge ahead,
That cuts through the rock,' he said,
'And at the head, there, of the dale,
Below you, you will see a vale;
My house is in the neighbourhood,
Between the water and the wood.'
So the youth rode, nor did he stop,
Yet when he came to the very top
He could see naught but earth and sky.
'Did I come here for this, say I?
God bring shame and foul disgrace
On him who sent me to this place!
Tis all a jest, twas all deceit.
I'd find a house there at my feet,
He said, if I but climbed to see;
A fine guide he turned out to be!
Good sir, you who told me this,
You indeed did me ill service,
If you misled me out of spite.'
Then, of a tower he caught sight;
Which in the valley, there, did root;
None finer this side of Beirut,
Nor better sited, would you find.
Square, and of brownstone mined,
Two smaller turrets flanked its sides.
And a hall fronted it, besides,
And lodgings lay before the hall.
The youth rode down towards it all,
Saying now, he'd served him well
Who'd sent him to that hidden dell.
And then towards the gate he wound,
Before the gate, a drawbridge found,

And it was lowered so any might
Ride over it; as did the knight;
And squires now ran to greet him,
Two came and helped disarm him;
A third then led his mount away,
To feed his horse on oats and hay;
A fourth brought him a mantle too,
Of scarlet cloth, all fresh and new;
Then to his lodgings led the knight
Who found his rooms a finer sight
Than any this side of Limoges,
Rooms fine enough to house the Doge.

LINES 3069-3152 THE FISHER KING GIFTS THE YOUTHA SWORD

THE youth was in his lodgings till
The lord of the castle spoke his will,
And two squires came then to escort
Him to the hall, and thus the court.
He found the hall was square inside,
For it was long as it was wide.
Amidst the hall, upon a bed,
Sat a lord, grey-haired his head,
And upon that head was set
A fine mulberry-black chaplet,
And the cap was made of sable,
Trimmed with the cloth, of purple,
From which his robe too was made.
Propped on an elbow there he lay;
And before him a fire was alight,
Of dry logs, and it burned bright,
Four pillars there, surrounding it.

And four hundred men could sit
Around that one enormous fire,
Each as warm as he might desire.
Those pillars were good and strong,
Supporting the hood above, of bronze,
The chimney-hood both tall and wide.
When the squires at the youth's side
Came before their lord, he stirred,
Greeting the young knight with a word:
'Friend, be you not displeased if I
Cannot stand to greet you, for I
Am unable to do so with ease.'
'By God, say naught, sire, if you please,
Of that; I mind not,' said the boy,
'If God yet grants me health and joy.'
The lord, such was his grievous pain,
Raised himself high on his bed again,
As best he could and: 'Friend,' he said,
'Be not dismayed, draw near the bed.
If you sat beside me, here, I should
View it favourably, an if you would.'
He sat near; then the lord did say:
'Now, friend, whence come you today?
'Sire, said the youth, this morn I came
From Beaurepaire; such is its name.'
'God save me,' said the nobleman,
Twas a long journey for any man
The journey you have made this day.
You must have started on your way
Ere the watch had called the dawn.'
'Twas, rather, the first hour of morn,
I do assure you,' said the lad.
While they this conversation had,
A squire entered through the door;
Slung from his neck, a sword he bore,

From a rich sword-belt it did hang;
He handed it to the nobleman,
Who drew it half-way from its sheath,
So he might see above, beneath,
Where twas made, for there twas writ,
By the maker when he fashioned it,
And that it was of such fine steel
It would not break he did reveal,
Except in one perilous event,
Only known to him who blent
The metals and had forged the sword.
The squire said: 'The maid, my lord,
Your niece, who is so good and fair,
Sends you this gift, and I declare
You'll not find one of such strength
For its given breadth and length.
Give the sword to whom you choose,
She'll be pleased if he shall use
It well, whom you do so reward,
For the one who forged the sword
Made but three, and now he dies;
He can forge no more, but lies
On his deathbed, this is his last.'
At once the lord the weapon passed
To the stranger, on him bestowed
The belt, the sheath, and its load,
For they formed a treasure, all told.
The pommel of the sword was gold,
Arabian or Greek the finish;
The gold-embroidered sheath from Venice.
This gift, and all so richly made,
The lord to the youth displayed,
And said: 'The sword that you see,
Yours was it destined thus to be,
May it aid you, now and alway;
Take it, and unsheathe it, pray.'

LINES 3153-3344 THE YOUTH HAS SIGHT OF THE GRAIL

HE thanked him, girding it on aright
Such that the belt was not too tight,
Then drew forth the naked blade,
And, gazing at it a little, then laid
It back in the scabbard once more.
He gazed at the sword, well he saw
It seemed at his side, as in his fist,
And looked as if it would assist
Him, at need, and most valiantly.
Behind him the squires he did see
Beside the brightly burning fire,
And so he turned towards the squire
Who kept his arms and commanded
He guard the sword, as he demanded.
Then he sat again, beside the lord.
Who him great honour did afford.
And the light there was as bright
As ever did shine the candlelight,
On a guest, in any house whatever.
They spoke of this and that together;
And from a room there came a squire,
And he passed by, between the fire
And bed, where sat the lord and knight,
And bore a lance of purest white
Holding it by the lance's centre,
And all those there saw him enter,
The white lance, its gleaming wood,
And from the tip the drop of blood
That issued forth, and from its end
Did to the squire's hand descend;

'The white lance, its gleaming wood,
And from the tip the drop of blood'
Adapted from Le Morte d'Arthur (1893), Sir Thomas Malory
(15th cent) and Ernest Rhys (1859-1946)
Internet Archive Book Images

Drop on drop, of pure vermilion.
The youth, who had but come upon
The place he was that very night,
Refrained from questioning outright
How this wonder had come about,
For he recalled, nor did he doubt,
The ruling Gournemant had taught,
That as a full-fledged knight he ought
To keep from speaking overmuch;
For ready questioning, as such,
Led swiftly in an ill direction.
So the youth asked no question.
Two more squires then appeared,
Candlestick in hand drew near.
Of gold, and inlaid with niello,
Were the candlesticks and, lo,
The squires they were passing fair;
And every candlestick borne there,
Ten lighted candles thus displayed.
And they were followed by a maid,
Fair, neat, and dressed with elegance,
Who bore a grail in her two hands;
And as she entered, on their tail,
And bearing in her hands the grail,
So great a brightness shone around,
And cast its light, the watchers found
The candlelight grow dim as, far
Off, dims the brightness of a star,
When the sun rises, or the moon.
After her, there followed soon
A maid who bore a silver plate.
The grail, which went ahead in state,
Was of pure gold, set with gems,
Such precious stones as diadems
Display, the richest to be found,

'And they were followed by a maid...
Who bore a grail in her two hands'
Le Morte d'Arthur (1893), Sir Thomas Malory (15th cent) and
Ernest Rhys (1859-1946)
Internet Archive Book Images

Beneath the sea, or underground;
Doubtless of much greater worth
Than all the other stones on earth,
The gems that from the grail shone.
From one room to another gone,
In the same manner as the lance,
Before their eyes all did advance.
And the youth, he saw them pass,
But of the grail, dared not, alas,
Ask: whom, with it, one served?
For, in his heart, he now observed
Ever, his wise teacher's warning.
I fear that woe, to him, twill bring;
For I've oft heard it said, that we
At once, may yet too silent be,
As, with this tongue of ours, too free;
If good it bring us, or ill we see,
I ask not, nor did he enquire.
The lord did then command a squire
To see they had napkins and water,
And those his request did further,
Who were accustomed to the task.
They of the lord and youth did ask,
Then in warm water laved their hands,
And next two squires, upon command,
Brought forth a table of ivory,
Which, or so relates the story,
Out of a single piece was made.
Before their lord twas displayed
Then they showed it to the lad;
Then two other squires, who had
Followed them, the trestles brought
Which acquired, when they were wrought,
The property that they would never
Perish, but would last forever.

For they were made of ebony,
Which has the property, you see,
That it will never rot or burn,
But those two things will ever spurn.
The table on that pair they set,
Nor did the tablecloth forget.
Of the cloth what shall I state?
No pope, cardinal, or legate,
Has dined with a whiter one.
The first course was venison,
A whole haunch, peppered, roasted;
And clear wine the table boasted,
In golden cups, a pleasant one.
A squire served the venison,
Carving it on the silver platter,
Into slices, and then the latter
Placing on whole rounds of bread.
Meanwhile the grail, as they fed,
Passed before the youth again,
And, of the grail, he did refrain
From asking: whom, with it, one served?
Thus he the warning still observed,
Which the lord had gently given
Against too much speech, unbidden,
One he remembered, in his heart.
Yet he proved too reticent by far.
At every course that was served
The grail's passage he observed,
In open view, and yet, reserved,
He knew not whom, with it, one served.
And yet, indeed, he wished to know,
And he would seek the truth, or so
He thought, lest he himself do wrong,
From some squire there, ere long;
Yet till the morning he would wait

'*Meanwhile the grail, as they fed,*
Passed before the youth again'
Le Morte d'Arthur (1893), Sir Thomas Malory (15th cent) and
Ernest Rhys (1859-1946)
Internet Archive Book Images

When he took leave, at the gate,
Of the lord and all his company;
And set the matter, quietly,
Aside, while they drank and ate.
Well-filled indeed was his plate,
Nor was the wine scarce at table;
Rather all proved delectable.
The dinner was both fair and fine.
Such a meal, such food and wine,
As king, and count, and emperor
Must eat, that night was served before
The lord and the knight, his guest.
Before they went to take their rest,
They sat there, and talked together,
While the squires, after the dinner,
Prepared the beds, served them fruit
And spices, the rarest kinds, to boot;
For pomegranates, figs, and dates,
Cloves, and nutmeg, graced the plates;
Herbs mixed with honey, before bed,
And Alexandrian gingerbread.
And spiced wine they drank; piment,
Without sweet honey or pepper blent;
Clear syrup; and mulberry liqueur.
The youth marvelled, more and more,
At things he knew not, without end;
Until the lord addressed him: 'Friend,
Tis time to retire now, for the night;
I go, but trouble not, sir knight,
I must lie down in my chamber,
Yet you may, all at your leisure,
Sleep in this room here, outside;
And the being-carried I must abide,
For, over my body, I've no power.'
Four servants issued, at that hour,

116

From a chamber and, as they met,
Each seized hold of the coverlet
By a corner, twas spread alway
Upon the bed where the lord lay;
Thus they bore him to his place.
Other servants, with good grace,
Aided the youth, and they indeed
Did minister to his every need.
They undressed him, when he chose,
Divested him of his shirt and hose,
And in white linen sheets he slept.
And till the morn his bed he kept,
Though the household woke at dawn;
All had risen to greet the morn.

Lines 3345-3409 The youth leaves with his questions unasked

He looked about him everywhere,
Yet, upon finding no one there,
Was forced to rise from bed alone.
And so, however he might moan,
Seeing he must, he rose from bed,
Having no choice when all was said,
And dressed alone, put on his shoes,
Took his armour, they did choose
To leave by the dais for him to find,
And armed himself again. Yet, mind,
Of what he'd brought he was bereft,
He donned the armour they had left.
When he had adorned his members,
He went out, toward those chambers,
He'd seen all oped the night before,

But closed he found was every door,
And so his wandering was in vain.
He shouted then he called again;
None opened there, or spoke a word.
When he'd ceased to call, unheard,
He went to the doorway of the hall,
Found it open, so, armour and all,
He thus descended the castle stair,
And found his horse, saddled, there,
And saw his shield, and his lance
Against the wall, and did advance,
And, mounting, looked on every side,
But not a soul did there abide,
Ne'er a single squire did he see.
He approached the gate, silently,
And there he found the drawbridge down,
Which the good people of the town
Had left thus lowered, I suppose,
So that, at any time he chose,
He could leave without delay.
He thought all the squires away
In the forest, all gone that day
By the bridge, to check their nets.
He cared not to wait, and yet,
Said to himself that he must go
To ask them if they might know
Of the lance that thus did bleed,
If they could tell of it, indeed,
And, of the grail, where it was borne.
So he rode on to greet the morn;
Yet before the bridge he'd cleared
His horses' front hooves appeared
To rise, and rise, till in the air
His horse leapt, and leapt full fair,
And had the horse not leapt so well

Both had fallen, yet neither fell,
Neither the steed nor he who rode.
And he looked back along the road,
Wondering how this was, amazed
To see the drawbridge had been raised,
And called aloud, yet none replied:
'You who raised the bridge' he cried
'Come you now, and speak with me!
Where are you that no eye can see?
Show yourself, grant me a view,
For there's a thing I'd ask of you
The answer to it I would know.'
But all his words were wasted so,
For none there replied, nor would.

LINES 3410-3519 THE MAID SPEAKS OF THE FISHER KING AND THE GRAIL

So he rode on towards the wood,
And entered on a path, and found
Horses' hooves had marked the ground,
Where riders had passed that way.
'This path,' he said 'they took this day,
Those squires whom I came to find.'
So through the woods he did wind,
While the hoof-prints he could see,
Till a maid, beneath a fine oak-tree,
He chanced upon, and she did moan,
And weep and wail there, and groan,
Like to some poor wretch in sorrow:
'Alas,' cried she, 'ill was the morrow,
And ill was that day when I was born,
That destined me to a life forlorn!

Nothing worse could come to me!
Would to God my love, that I see,
And hold here in my arms, dead,
He'd preserved from death instead.
His death makes me to weep and pine.
Would that he lived, and death was mine!
Why take his soul, yet mine remains?
What is life worth, with all its pains,
When all that I loved here lies dead?
Without him I care naught, instead,
For this my life, or this my body.
Death, now snatch my soul from me,
To be a handmaid that would fain
Accompany his, if he so deign.'
Tears from her eyes she expelled,
For a knight whose corpse she held,
Whose head had been severed clean.
The youth, her sorrow having seen,
Halted not till he was before her,
Then he stopped and saluted her,
And she him with her head bowed;
Yet did not cease to weep aloud.
And the youth said: 'Who did harm
To the knight who lies in your arms,
Demoiselle? Sire, twas a knight,'
Said the maid, 'on this very morn.
Yet I marvel; you might rise at dawn,
God save me and my witness be
To this wonder that here I see,
And thirty-five leagues straight
Ride the way you came of late,
Before you ere might come upon
Lodgings, honest, clean, that one
Might find good; and yet your steed
Has gleaming flanks, as if indeed,

He'd been groomed at some inn,
And fed on oats and hay within,
Washed and brushed, for his coat
Could not be glossier, his throat,
His neck, nor he look better fed.
And you too, risen from some bed,
Or so it seems to me, fair knight,
Where you found rest and ease last night.'
'T'faith, fair lady, and to my mind,
The best I might I there did find,
And if I show it tis only right.
If any were to shout outright
Now, from here, where we are,
They'd hear it there, tis not far,
There, where I did pass the night.
You cannot truly have had sight
Of all this land, nor traversed all.
I had lodgings, I thus recall,
That are the finest I have known.'
'Ah, fair sire, then do you own
That you did find such fine lodging,
At the castle of the Fisher King?'
'Maid, by the Saviour, I know not
If he's king, fisherman, or what,
But he's most wise and courteous.
I can but say, last eve it was
Two men I saw, and in one boat,
Which gently down the stream did float.
One man chose the course it took,
The other fished, with line and hook,
He spoke of his house, where I might
Find lodgings, as I did, last night.'
And the maiden said: 'Fair sire,
He is a king, for I am no liar,
But in a battle he was maimed,

Wounded sorely, and so lamed
That naught is to be done at all.
The wound that did him befall?
A javelin pierced both his thighs,
And the pain doth him chastise,
Such that he cannot mount a horse,
Yet when he would have recourse
To sport or pleasure, in a boat
He is placed, and then, afloat,
Fish to his hook he doth bring;
Thus he's called the Fisher King,
And that pleasure is his delight;
For there is naught else, sir knight,
That he may suffer or endure.
He cannot hunt now as before,
But huntsmen, wild-fowlers too,
Falconers, archers, not a few,
He has, to scour his realm for game.
So he is pleased, though he is lame,
To remain there in his retreat.
For in all the world, there's no seat
So benefits him, and nowhere
Suits him as well, so tis there
Was built his house fit for a king.'

LINES 3520-3639 SHE QUESTIONS THE YOUTH, WHOSE TRUE NAME IS PERCEVAL

'T' FAITH, there's truth in everything,'
Replied the youth, 'that you do say.
I saw such wonders, yesterday;
As I stood at a distance there,
When to his hall I did repair,

He told me I should draw near,
And sit by him and, lest it appear
Twas from pride he failed to rise
And greet me, I should realise
He could not do so, and, at that,
Seeing he lacked the power, I sat.'
'Surely, he did you great honour,
To seat you there in that manner!
And when you were seated there,
Say if you saw, and were aware
Of the lance, from which blood drains,
Though it has neither flesh nor veins?'
'Did I see? Yes, i'faith, did I.'
'And then, fair sire, did you ask why
It bled.' 'No, I asked naught at all.'
'God save me then, whate'er befall,
You worked ill, that you did so fail.
Now tell me, did you see the grail?
'Yes, indeed.' 'And who held it near?'
'A maid.' 'From whence did she appear?'
'From a room she came; she did go
Into another, and passed me so.'
'And the grail, did any go before?
'Yes.' 'And who?' 'Two squires, no more.'
'In their hands, what were they holding?'
Candlesticks, full of candles glowing.'
'And behind the grail, what came after?
'A maid.' 'And what held she before her?'
'She held a little silver plate.'
'And did you not ask, or soon or late,
Where it was they were going to?'
'Naught from my lips did so issue.'
'So much the worse; and God defend
Me, and have you a name, my friend?'
And he, who knew not his true name,

'*Now tell me, did you see the grail?*'
Le Morte d'Arthur (1893), Sir Thomas Malory (15th cent) and
Ernest Rhys (1859-1946)
Internet Archive Book Images

Divined it, saying from Wales he came,
And Perceval the Welshman was he,
Not knowing if he spoke truthfully;
Yet spoke true, though he knew it not.
And the maiden then, on hearing what
He'd said, rose up, from him who'd died,
And, as if in anger, she replied:
'Your name is changed.' 'How?' said he.
'Now Perceval the Wretched be!
Ah, Perceval, the unfortunate,
What grave mischance has marred your fate;
That all you saw you failed to question!
For if you had but sought direction,
You'd have healed the crippled king,
Renewed the use of both his limbs,
And he'd have trod his realm again.
And great good would we have gained!
But now, you must know, ill will fall
On you, and on others cast its pall.
For your sin against your mother,
It ensues, and against no other,
For through you she died of grief.
I know you better, tis my belief,
Than you do me, for you know not
That I too am of your line begot;
For your mother's house, that same,
Raised both; I, your cousin germain.
I grieve no less that you did fail
To seek to learn about the grail,
What is done with it, where tis borne,
Than for your mother I do mourn,
Nor, indeed, for this knight here
Whom I loved and held most dear,
And most for this, that he called me
His own dear friend, and guided me

As should a frank and loyal knight.'
'Ah, cousin, if you speak aright,'
Said Perceval, 'and all this is so,
Then tell me how it is you know.'
'I know she's dead,' the maid replied,
'As truly as those men who sighed
And placed her body in the ground.'
'May God, for his goodness renowned,
Have mercy on her soul,' said he.
'An ill tale have you told to me.
And since she is beneath the earth,
What then is further effort worth?
For I was journeying for naught
Except to see her whom I sought.
Now I must choose another road.
But if with me you now would go
I am most willing; he, who here
Lies dead, can aid you not, I fear;
The living to the living,' he said,
'And likewise, the dead to the dead!
Let us go, you and I, together.
For tis folly and no other,
It seems to me, that you, alone,
Should guard the dead, and make moan.
Let us go seek him who did slay
Your love and if, upon the way,
I meet with him, I pledge,' said he,
'I'll conquer him, or he'll slay me.'
And she who could not supress
Her grief and her heart's distress,
Replied: 'Sire, there is no way
That I can go with you this day,
Nor leave him ere he is interred.
If you trust in me then, in a word,
Go you that way, the paved road,

For that way too the fell knight rode,
That proud knight who, so cruelly,
Has taken my sweet love from me.
And yet I don't say that because
I'd have yourself take that course
God help me, and pursue him still;
Though I do wish him every ill,
As if twere my own self he'd slain.

LINES 3640-3676 THE MAID SPEAKS OF PERCEVAL'S SWORD

BUT the sword, how did you gain
That weapon, hung at your left side,
That ne'er drew blood, nor man defied,
Nor e'er was drawn in time of need?
I know where it was forged, indeed
I know the hand that forged it too.
Take care, and trust it not, for you
That blade will utterly betray;
Amidst the battle, on that day,
Suddenly, twill break to pieces.'
'My cousin, one of the fair nieces
Of my kind host, sent it last eve
To him, and he gave it to me.
I thought it a fine gift, but nay,
Now it fills me with dismay
If all that you have said is true.
Tell me if you know, say you,
If this blade should ever break,
Could any smith the sword remake?'
'Yes, but great pains must he take.
Who knows the road to the lake
That lies beyond Cotouatre,

He might have the blade, thereafter,
Re-forged, and tempered, and made so.
If you should venture thus to go,
Then seek for none but Trebuchet,
The smith who forged it, on a day;
He made, and could remake it true,
As never another smith could do,
That you might meet with anywhere.
That no other so attempt, have care;
They'll not succeed, tis my belief.'
'Indeed, it would bring me grief,'
Said Perceval, 'were it to break.'
She watched, as he his way did take,
Not wishing from the dead to part,
For whom she grieved in her heart.

Lines 3677-3812 A damsel in distress

PERCEVAL sped on, like a hound
Hot on the trail, until he found
A palfrey, so bone-tired and thin,
Treading the path in front of him,
So thin and wretched a creature,
It seemed in the course of nature
To have fallen into evil hands,
Subject to one and all's demands,
Ill-cared for, as if it had, indeed,
Been nothing but a hired steed,
Labouring in the hours of light,
And much neglected overnight.
Such it was the palfrey seemed.
It shivered so you might have deemed
Half-frozen twas, the trembling horse,

Or feverish, and the mane, perforce,
Long vanished, ears drooping low;
Fit but to feed the dogs, although
The hounds and the mongrels would
Find only skin and bones, not blood,
Since only skin the bones did hide.
On its back, a saddle did reside,
On its head, a bridle did sag,
Such as were suited to the nag;
A maiden rode it, and made moan,
None more wretched ever known,
Yet she would have passed for fair
If she'd known better fortune there.
But she was then in such distress,
That not a palm's breadth of her dress
Was whole, and then through the rips
Her breasts both displayed their tips.
With clumsy stitches here and there
The garment was sewn and patched;
Her skin too had been badly scratched,
By hail, and scorched by snow and frost.
Her hair hung loose, her veil was lost,
Thus, all exposed, appeared her face,
And it was marked by many a trace
Of tears that each had left its stain
As they fell, ceaselessly, like rain,
And trickled down to wet her breast
The garment in which she was dressed,
And all its cloth, down to her knees.
But sadder still than were all these
Was her heart, its weight of care.
As soon as Perceval saw all there,
He rode at full speed towards her,
While she sought to draw together
Her torn dress, to hide her better;

Though the holes seemed rather
Bent on growing, and moreover
As she sought each hole to cover,
Another hundred opened wide.
Pale and wretched thus, she sighed
And moaned, as Perceval drew near,
Bewailing, he could not but hear,
Her suffering, her loss of ease:
'Lord,' said she, 'if it but please,
Let me not live in long duress!
Long I've endured wretchedness,
Yet these, my ills, are undeserved!
Too ill a fate's for me reserved!
Lord, you know that I have not
Merited all that seems my lot,
So, God, send me, if you know,
Someone who might ease my woe,
Or deliver me from him I blame,
Who makes me to live in shame.
He shows such small mercy to me,
That I shall not, alive, go free;
And yet he wills not I should die,
And I know not the reason why
He seeks my company this way,
Unless some pleasure now it may
Grant him, my shame and misery.
Yet if he knew, and knew truly,
That I'd, indeed, deserved it all,
Then his mercy on me should fall,
Now that I have paid so dearly,
If I had pleased him, yet clearly
He loves me not at all, when he
Forces me to live so harshly,
Following him, and he cares not.'
'God save you, lady, from your lot!'

Cried Perceval, now at her side,
And hearing him, she thus replied,
Hiding herself, voice soft and low:
'Fair sire, who doth greet me so,
May your heart's desire be granted,
Though your greeting is unwanted.'
Perceval, who blushed with shame,
Responded to her words of blame:
'Halt then, my lady, tell me why?
For, at no time, I think, have I
Seen you before, nor in any way
Done wrong to you ere this day.'
'Yes, you have,' she said, 'for I
Am so wretched, so gone awry,
That none should give me greeting.
I sweat with anguish on meeting
All who detain, or gaze at, me.'
'I was not yet aware, most truly,'
Said Perceval, 'of that mischance.
For I'd no intent, at this instance,
To cause you shame, nor this day
Came so to do; I chanced this way.
Yet since I see you weeping there
In such wretchedness, poor and bare,
No joy will I have, in my heart
If you do not now, for your part,
Say what has caused you such pain
And sorrow, as you now sustain.'
'Ah, fair sire, have mercy on me!
Be silent now, for you must flee
And leave me here alone, in peace.
You do wrong, for you must cease
To linger; flee, if you'd be wise.'
'If so,' said he, 'I'd be apprised
Of what threat, or from what abuse,

I should flee, where none pursues?'
'From the Proud Knight of the Wood,
Who asks naught, tis understood,
Except the melee and the fight,
Or encountering some knight,
And who if he finds you here
Must surely slay you, I fear.
He hates it if I rest at all,
And none departs intact withal,
Who lingers thus to talk with me,
Should he arrive in time; you see,
He takes from every man his head,
And he, before he strikes them dead,
Tells each man why, with cruelty,
He worries and chastises me.'

LINES 3813-3899 THE PROUD KNIGHT OF THE WOOD

WHILE they talked, as any would,
The Proud Knight issued from the wood,
And came much like a lightning thrust
From thence, in clouds of sand and dust.
Crying: 'You there, beside the maid,
Twas ill in truth when you waylaid
Her; know you that your end is come,
In that you made her halt, for some
Few steps, perchance, or only one.
Yet I'll not slay you, ere I'm done
Telling you the reason why
For what crime, what misdeed I
Make the maid endure such shame.
Listen, and you'll hear the same.
One day to the wood I was gone,

And behind, in my pavilion,
I'd left this maiden, whom I loved
More than all the stars above;
When, riding through the wood, there came
A Welshman; I know not his name,
Nor where he went to, after this,
But ere he went he stole a kiss
From her, by force, or so she said;
And if she lied, what then, instead?
Once he'd kissed her; despite his will
Would he not, then, have had her still?
Yes, indeed, none would believe
That he could simply kiss and leave,
Since one thing leads to another.
He who kisses and does no other,
When they are one on one, alone,
The choice is his, if all be known.
A woman who doth not protest
At the kiss, soon grants the rest,
Tis what she doth herself intend,
And though herself she doth defend
Tis known to all, without a doubt,
A woman would win every bout
Except that one melee of note
Where she grabs him by the throat,
Scratches, bites, and seeks to kill,
For she would be vanquished still,
Though she defends and doth delay.
Too cowardly to yield the day,
She wishes force to take its place,
Though he ingratitude will face.
And so I think he lay with her.
And took my ring, as I discover,
Which she wore upon her finger.
His taking it has fuelled my anger.

But ere he did he drank my wine,
And ate of three good pasties, mine;
The three were being kept for me.
So now a fine reward has she,
This lass of mine, as all can see.
Let them pay who yield to folly,
So they'll not care to sin again.
I was full mad with anger then,
When of the truth I had sight.
Furious, what I did was right:
Her palfrey would not be fed
On oats, nor groomed, I said,
Nor be re-shod; and what she wore,
The cloak and tunic from before,
She should wear, until that hour
When I'd have him in my power
Who'd forced her, until he'd bled
In battle, and I'd won his head.'
When Perceval had heard him out
He replied, turn and turn about:
'Friend, know this truth, for one,
She has more than penance done,
For I am the man who kissed her,
By force, and so much grieved her,
And from her finger took the ring
But did, and had, no other thing;
Though I did eat, I must confess,
One pasty and a half, no less,
And drank as much wine as I would,
Yet wisely, not all that I could.'
'Upon my life, the knight replied,
'The whole thing has me stupefied,
Tis a fine meal now that you serve!
Death you, assuredly, deserve,
If your confession is but true.'

'My death is not so near; be you'
Said Perceval, 'assured of that!'

LINES 3900-3976 THE PROUD KNIGHT, DEFEATED, IS SENT TO ARTHUR'S COURT

AND having dealt, thus, tit for tat,
Without more words, each spurred his steed
At the foe, so furiously indeed
They made splinters of their lances,
To the earth made their advances,
As from their saddles they were thrown.
But both leapt to their feet, I own,
And trusted to the naked blade,
And mighty blows each other paid.
The battle was both long and hard.
Of that no more, so says the bard,
To yield it time were time wasted,
Except to say that both men tasted
Enough of it, for the Proud Knight
To cry mercy, and, as was right,
Perceval, who had ne'er forgot
The lord who'd advised him not
To slay any knight who'd lost
And mercy sought, at any cost,
Declared: 'No mercy yet is due
To you sir knight, I'faith, till you
Show some mercy to your friend,
For she has not, you may depend
Upon it, deserved the sorry ill,
That you make her suffer still.'
As she was the apple of his eye,
'Fair sire, I will,' was his reply,

'I'll make amends as you advise.
There is no task you can devise
That I'm unwilling to perform;
My heart is sad at all the storm
Of grief and woe I've made her bear.'
'Go to your nearest dwelling, where
The maid can bathe herself and rest,
And be your manners of the best,
Till she is fully healed, and well;
Then, dressed in her best apparel,
Let her be led to Arthur's court,
Greet the king for me; and sport
The same armour you now wear,
And go seek out his mercy there.
If he demands whence you come,
Say tis from the same lad whom
He made a knight, armed in red,
Thanks to the wise and prudent head
Of my Lord Kay the Seneschal.
And there repeat to one and all,
The penance that your maid did bear;
Go tell the king, the courtiers there,
Your tale, the queen, and every maid
Of whom she leads a fine brigade.
And I prize one, fair and lovely,
Who was, because she smiled at me,
Dealt by Sir Kay a vicious blow
That nigh on stunned the maiden so.
Seek her out, such is my command,
And tell her, she will understand,
That I'll not enter, not for aught,
The hallows of King Arthur's court,
Until I have avenged that blow;
Which she'll be overjoyed to know.'
And he declared that he would go,

Most willingly, and tell her so.
His words he'd faithfully convey,
And do so without more delay
Than was needed for them to rest,
His maid be well, and be dressed,
And they equipped with all required;
And, he declared, he much desired
That Perceval lodge there, and rest,
To treat his wounds, twould be best,
Until his cuts and bruises healed.
'Go, may fate good fortune yield,'
Said Perceval, 'keep her in mind;
For other lodgings I shall find.'

LINES 3977-4053 THE PROUD KNIGHT TELLS HIS TALE AT COURT

THEIR talk thus ended for the day,
Both the knights brooked no delay,
And left, as swiftly as they might.
The one who'd lost, that very night,
Had his lover bathed, and dressed
And with such care was she blessed
To her full beauty she returned.
Then to the journey there they turned,
And to Carlion took their road,
Where King Arthur had his abode,
And he held a feast now, privily,
For he'd gathered there but three
Thousand worthy knights of note,
To them his presence did devote.
The knight entered Arthur's court,
With his lover whom he'd brought,

And rendered himself his prisoner,
Before him did this speech deliver:
'I'm here as your prisoner, sire,
To be dealt with as you desire,
Which is reasonable and right,
So commanded by that knight
Who crimson armour asked of you,
And then fought, and won it too.'
On hearing this, King Arthur knew
The matter he alluded to:
'Remove your armour now, fair sire,
May he who sends you thus to me
Find fortune, and right joyous be.
Be welcome, for we hold you dear,
And you shall be most honoured here.'
'Sire, one thing more he asked of me,
And this much I would ask of thee,
Ere I disarm, that the queen be here,
And her ladies, that they might hear
The substance of this further thing
This message I was asked to bring,
Which requires the presence though,
Of the maid who was dealt a blow
For a smile she gave, on a time,
And twas, that smile, her only crime.'
Here the Proud Knight's speech ended.
The king hearing the thing depended
On the queen's presence, sent for her;
She came and all her maids, together,
They hand in hand, and two by two,
So they might hear the message too.
When the queen was seated beside
Her lord, King Arthur, the knight cried:
'Lady, his greetings one doth send,
One upon whom you may depend,

Who is a knight I prize, for he
By force of arms defeated me.
Of him I know no more to tell
But that he sends this maid as well,
To you, this friend I have beside me.'
'I thank him then, my friend' said she.
And then the knight retold that same
Tale of cruelty and shame,
You have heard, how for so long
She'd felt the weight of his wrong.
And hiding naught, but with a sigh,
He yielded all, and the reason why.
After his speech, they pointed out
The maid whom Kay had dealt a clout,
And the knight said: 'He who sent
Me here, lass, said that his intent
Was that I greet you now from him,
Nor loose the boots from my limbs,
Until I've said that not for aught
Will he enter King Arthur's court,
So help him God, till he's repaid
The blow, the shame upon you laid,
That you, for him, were forced to bear.'

LINES 4054-4123 KING ARTHUR DETERMINES
TO FIND THE YOUTH

AND then the fool leapt in the air,
At all he'd heard, and he did cry:
'God bless me, Lord Kay, say I,
An you will pay the price, truly,
And it will be soon, most surely.'
After the fool, then spoke the king:

'Ah, Kay, twas a discourteous thing
You did when you mocked the youth!
It was your mockery, in truth,
That drove him from me, forever.'
And then the knight, his prisoner,
The king made to sit before him,
And, freeing the knight, had him
Stripped of armour, at his command.
And he who sat at his right hand,
My Lord Gawain, did now enquire:
'In God's name, then who is he, sire,
Who has conquered, by arms alone,
As good a knight as e'er was known?
Through all the Isles in the sea,
I've never yet had named to me
Nor e'er seen a knight or known,
A peer to this knight here, I own,
In feats of arms or chivalry.'
'His name it is unknown to me,
Dear nephew, replied the king.'
'I saw him, yet asked not a thing
Of him, nor his name, I confess,
For he of me did make request
To dub him, on the spot, a knight,
I thought him noble, at first sight,
And said, thus: "Brother, willingly;
Do you dismount, and instantly,
Until here we may have brought
Gilded arms such as you sought."
And he replied that he would not
Tread the ground, until he'd got
The crimson arms he coveted.
He'd have no other arms, he said,
His words stunning us outright,
But those sported by that knight

Who stole the golden cup from us.
Then Kay, who was discourteous,
And is, and will be so alway,
Who never good doth seek or say,
Cried: 'Brother the king grants you
That armour, you may take it too!'
The lad who thought he meant it
Chased the knight and, in a minute,
Killed him with a javelin throw.
Though if you ask I do not know
How the combat thus began,
But the Knight in Vermilion
From the wood of Quinqueroi,
I know not why, struck the boy,
With his lance, all in his pride.
And thus, all proudly, he died,
Struck by the javelin, in the eye,
And, to the lad, arms did supply.
He's served me so well, since then,
By Saint David, to whom the men
And the women of Wales do pray,
I'll not abide more than a day
Or sleep two nights together
In the selfsame hall or chamber,
Till I know he lives; on land or sea,
Rather, I'll seek him endlessly.'
And when they heard the king so swear
They knew, all those who were there,
That, he would truly seek him so.

Lines 4124-4193 The falcon, the wild goose, and the drops of blood

Then you'd have seen them go
Fill the chests, and naught forget,
Not one sheet, pillow, or coverlet,
And burden the pack horses too,
And load the wagons, not a few;
So many the tents and canopies,
A well-lettered clerk might seize
His pen, and write all day, and yet
Not tally all, nor the sum be met
Of all they'd packed so rapidly.
Then the king departed swiftly,
From Carlion, and there behind
Rode all his barons, nor, you'd find
Did one handmaiden still remain;
All followed in the queen's train,
To show her power and majesty.
That night in the fields did he
Set up his camp, beside a wood.
And that night snow fell, to hood
The land with its chill canopy.
Perceval, that morn, rose early
As he was wont to do, a knight
Who always wished to alight
Upon chivalry and adventure;
And he chanced, at a venture,
On that field where the king's tent
Was with snow and frost all blent.
But ere he came that tent before
A flock of wild geese he saw

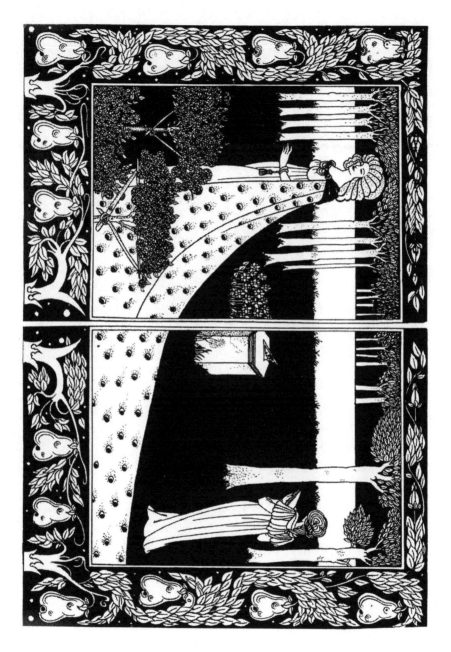

'*All followed in the queen's train,*
To show her power and majesty'
Le Morte d'Arthur (1893), Sir Thomas Malory (15th cent) and
Ernest Rhys (1859-1946)
Internet Archive Book Images

That had been dazzled by the snow.
He saw them and heard them, low
Above the ground, all flying
From a falcon that came crying
After them, at breakneck speed,
Till it spied one bird, indeed,
Separate from all the others,
Struck hard at the tail feathers,
Knocking the bird to the ground;
But proved too tardy, as it found,
Flew off, and failed to seize its prey.
Perceval swiftly made his way
To the place where he saw it fall.
The goose, wounded scarce at all,
Let fall, there, three drops of blood,
That dyed the snow, as if it could
Have been so tinted by nature.
So unharmed was the creature
That, when awhile it had lain
Where it was downed, it once again
Took to the air and flew away.
But Perceval say the disarray
Of the snow, where it had been,
And the blood still to be seen,
Where he leant upon his lance.
He well-nigh fell into a trance,
As it revealed the fresh colour
That graced the face of his lover,
For there he felt, in plain sight,
The crimson offset the white,
As these drops of blood had so
Dyed the whiteness of the snow;
And his mind as thus he gazed
Was with delight so fair amazed,
Dreaming twas the colour there

Of the face of his love so fair.
Perceval mused, and thus did eye
The blood all morn, till, by and by,
The king's squires issued from the tent
And seeing him there, all intent
On his vision, thought him sleeping.

LINES 4194-4247 SIR SAGRAMORE CHALLENGES THE YOUTH

THOUGH the king was still slumbering,
Where he lay, quietly, in his bed,
The squires encountered, instead
Before the king's grand pavilion,
Where there was scarcely anyone,
Sir Sagramore, the Impetuous,
Or called such by the cautious.
'Whence is it, you squires scurry?
Now, hide naught, why the hurry?'
'Sire, over there we saw a knight
Sleeping on his horse, upright.'
'And is he armed?' 'He is i'faith.'
'Then I'll go speak to him, i'faith,
And I shall bring him to the court.'
Sagramore then went and sought
The king's bed, and woke the king.
'Sire, there's a knight slumbering
Outside,' said he, 'in the open field.'
The king his command did yield,
That Sagramore should swiftly go
Speak to the knight, plead, and so
Bring him to them, in due course.
So Sagramore called for his horse,
And said to bring his armour on,

And what he asked, that was done;
Thus he was soon armed indeed,
And, fully armed, spurred his steed,
And rode out, towards the knight:
'Sire, now you must come, of right,
To the court.' He spoke not a word,
The knight, as if he had not heard;
So Sagramore, he spoke again;
Silent the knight did still remain.
'By Saint Peter,' Sagramore cried,
'You shall come, I'll not be denied!
To sit here, and to plead with you,
That angers me; my words to you
Have proven thus but ill-employed!'
Then lance and pennant he deployed,
And on the field he took his stance,
And warned the knight he would advance
And strike him should he not beware.
Perceval looked towards him there,
And saw a fight was what he sought,
And so, emerging from his thought,
The knights met violently together.
As they encountered one another,
Sagramore's lance broke in two,
But Perceval's followed through,
And struck the knight with such force
It sent him tumbling from his horse,
While the steed, its head held high,
Sped on, and from the field did fly,
At full gallop, towards the tents.

LINES 4248-4345 KAY CHALLENGES THE YOUTH
AND HIS ARM IS BROKEN

THE barons, knowing what it meant
To see the empty saddle, muttered.
But Kay who scarcely ever uttered
A kind word, cried out, jeeringly,
To the king: 'Fair Sire, now see,
How Sagramore returns to you;
The knight held by the bridle too,
He leads him here against his will!'
'Kay,' said the king, 'you do ill
In sneering at true gentlemen.
Go you there, and do better then
Than Sir Sagramore, if you can.'
'Sire,' said Kay, ''tis pleased I am
That you, sire, would have me go.
By force, whether he will or no,
I'll bring him here, the very same,
And I shall make him tell his name.'
Then he armed himself, carefully,
And armed, and mounted, thus did he
Go towards the knight who gazed
On three drops of blood, so mazed,
He gave no thought to other things.
He heard not Kay's loud bellowing
From afar: 'Fellow, attend the king!
You will go there, or I shall bring
You, and you shall pay most dearly.'
Perceval, now he heard more clearly
Kay's menaces, wheeled his mount,
And with steel spurs gave account

Of his intent; and the horse sped on,
So that the two knights met head on,
Each longing to display his skill;
Each rode, as if he aimed to kill.
Kay struck as hard as he could,
But his lance broke like rotten wood,
While Perceval, gathering no moss,
Struck Kay above his shield boss,
Hurling him against a boulder,
So as to dislocate his shoulder,
And twixt it and the elbow there
Break the bone, and him impair,
Indeed it snapped like a dry stick;
Just as the Fool divined, full quick
What the Fool divined was done;
Proven true was his divination.
Kay fainted away in sore distress,
While his horse did flight address,
Galloping away towards his tent.
The Britons knew what it meant:
The horse, but not the Seneschal.
Squires ran, on the reins to haul,
And the knights and ladies stirred.
When of his fainting they all heard
They feared lest he might be dead.
The king was most discomforted,
And they were grieved one and all.
But on the three drops that did fall,
Perceval, propped upon his lance,
Returned to gaze, as if in trance,
The Seneschal was only wounded;
Now the king was greatly angered,
But the lords said: be not dismayed,
For Kay would heal, with the aid
Of a doctor who knew how to set

The collarbone in place, and let
The broken arm repair correctly.
And the king who cared dearly
For Kay, and loved him, at heart,
Sent a doctor, skilled in his art,
And three maidens, trained by him,
Who reset the collarbone for him,
And so strapped the broken arm
The bone would knit, without harm.
They carried Kay to the king's tent,
And comforted him, on solace bent,
And said no sorrow should he feel,
For he'd be well, and swiftly heal.
My Lord Gawain said to the king:
'Sire, it is but a sorry thing,
God save me, as you well know,
For you yourself have told us so,
Always, and have judged aright,
For others to disturb a knight
As these two have, when deep in thought
Upon any matter; and for naught.
Whether they've done wrong or not,
I cannot say, but grief's their lot,
And great mishap, most certainly.
The knight mayhap, it seems to me,
Was thinking on some loss of his,
Or his lover whom he doth miss,
He was so troubled, ill at ease.
But I will go and, if it please,
View the knight's countenance
And if I find, when I advance,
That his thoughts now are bright,
I will then request the knight
Comes and attends upon you here.'

LINES 4346-4393 GAWAIN GOES TO SPEAK TO THE YOUTH

AT this, Kay angered did appear
And said: 'Ah, my Lord Gawain
No doubt by his hand you'll be fain
To take him, though ill he vows!
You'll do well, if he so allows,
And thereby concedes the fight.
So you've taken many a knight.
When the man was good and tired,
And a swift abatement he desired,
Then of the king you asked leave
His prompt surrender to receive!
Gawain, rain curses on my head,
If you're any man's fool, instead
We should take lessons from you!
You know the art of speaking too,
In words both pleasant and polite.
Would you e'er say, to a knight,
Things haughty, irritating, vile?
Those we know we would revile
Who'd think it, or e'er thought so!
In a silken gown you could go
To conduct this whole affair,
And never be obliged to bear
A sword now, or break a lance.
You only need seize your chance,
Get your tongue round a word or two,
Such as: "Fair sire, God save you,
And keep you alive and healthy,"
He'll do your bidding instantly.
There is naught for you to learn,

Compliments are yours to turn,
You'll stroke him as one strokes a cat,
And all will say: 'In dire combat
My Lord Gawain fought manfully!'
'Ah, Sir Kay, more courteously
You might speak to me,' he said.
'Will you vent your spleen on my head,
Treat me to your maliciousness?
Fair sweet friend, I will address
This matter, i'faith, and yet own
To no dislocated collarbone,
Or broken arm, as some today,
For, indeed, I like not such pay.'
'Nephew, go now,' said the king,
'You've said many a courteous thing;
If you can do so, bring the knight
But go you armed, as if to fight,
For defenceless you shall not go.'

LINES 4394-4509 GAWAIN BRINGS PERCEVAL TO THE KING

GAWAIN was armed, and swiftly so,
Whom, for his every virtue, they
Praised and prized, and straight away
Mounted a strong and willing steed,
And rode to the knight, at full speed,
Who leaning there, upon his lance,
Proved neither weary in his stance
Nor of his thoughts, where every one
Pleased him still, although the sun
Had melted two of the blood stains
That blent with the snow their remains,
And now the third was vanishing,

So that though absorbed in musing
He was not quite so entranced.
And my Lord Gawain advanced
Towards him at an ambling pace,
Nor threat nor anger in his face,
And said: 'Sire, I'd have hailed you
Had I known your heart as I do
My own, and yet this I may say
I come to meet you here today
As a messenger of the king,
And, from him, a request I bring
That you will go and speak with him.'
'Two have already come from him,
Said Perceval, 'who thus disturbed
My pleasure, and would have curbed
My freedom, by leading me away;
For I was deep in thought, I say,
Thought that offered me delight,
And those two, who wished to blight
My liberty, sought not my good.
Three crimson drops of fresh blood
Lay there before me on the snow;
And twas illumined by their glow,
And, gazing there, it seemed to me
That in those colours I did see
The fresh hues of my lady's face,
And would rest ever in that place.'
'Indeed, sire' said my Lord Gawain,
'Such thoughts as these, I would maintain
Are far from base, but rare and sweet;
Brutes and fools those who compete
To draw your heart from such musing.
Yet I long to know this simple thing:
What you might wish, that being so;
For I would willingly have you go

See the king, should it not grieve you.'
'First, tell me, sire, or e'er we do,
And tell me true,' said Perceval
If Kay be there, the Seneschal?'
'Yes, he is there, indeed tis true,
For he but now fought with you,
And that fight it did him harm,
For it has broken his right arm,
And put awry his collarbone.'
'Then the maid's avenged, I own,'
Cried Perceval, 'whom Kay struck.'
These words of his, so uttered, took
Gawain aback; amazed, he cried:
'God save me, for the king doth ride
In search of you, tis why he came.
Sire, may I ask of you your name?'
'Perceval am I; and you are, sire?'
'Know then that I, tis your desire,
Was given, when baptised, the name
Of Gawain.' 'Gawain?' 'Yes, the same.'
Perceval joyed at what he heard,
And said: 'Fair sire, many a word
Of you I've heard in many a place,
And I would have we two embrace
In friendship, such I'd ask of you,
If you but chose to seek it too.'
'Indeed,' replied my Lord Gawain,
'An twould please me no less to gain
Such friendship than twould you, withal;
More, I believe.' 'Then,' Perceval
Cried: 'I'faith, I will go with you,
Willingly, tis right and proper too;
And greater esteem doth me attend
That I may call myself your friend.'
Then each the other did embrace,

And then they started to unlace
Each his helmet and his ventail,
And free his head from the mail.
They left the spot, in great delight,
And the squires who witnessed knight
Clasp knight together thus, in joy,
From a hillside, did their legs employ,
And ran at once to tell the king:
'Sire, sire, Lord Gawain is coming,
I'faith, he brings the knight to you,'
They cried, 'and they do show, those two,
The greatest joy in one another.'
There was not one who did discover
The news, and failed to leave the tent,
And rush to be there at that event.
And Kay said to his lord, the king:
'Thus all the honour in this thing
Goes to your nephew, Sir Gawain;
Hard went the battle, that is plain,
And perilous twas, assuredly,
For he returns of hurt as free
As when he went, I perceive,
And not one blow did he receive,
And no one had of him a blow,
And not one word of challenge; lo
By him are all the honours won,
And let all cry that he has done
What we two could ne'er achieve,
Though we showed there, I believe
All our prowess, and all our might!'
Thus Kay delivered, wrong or right,
His judgment there, as was his wont.

LINES 4510-4578 PERCEVAL MAKES HIMSELF KNOWN TO ALL

Now Lord Gawain who did not want
To bring his new companion armed
Before the court, had him disarmed
By his own squires, within his tent,
And then his chamberlain was sent
To bring a robe from out his coffer
Which he to Perceval did offer.
When he was dressed, in finery,
Both cloak and tunic artfully
Sewn, and suiting him full well,
They went, hand in hand, to tell
The king, who was before his tent,
Of their meeting: 'Sire, I present
To you,' declared my Lord Gawain,
'The very one, whom you would fain
Have met, most willingly, I trow,
This past fortnight, and I avow
Tis he of whom you often speak,
And whom you now go to seek.
I offer him to you, him I bring.'
'My thanks to you,' declared the king,
Fair nephew,' and, so as to greet
Them both, he rose now to his feet.
And said: 'Fair sire, be welcome here!
I'd have you say, that all might hear,
What name you'd have me call you by.'
'T'faith, I shall hide naught, not I,'
Said Perceval,' and thus comply:
Perceval the Welshman am I.'
'Ah, Perceval, my dear sweet friend,

155

Since my court you'll now attend,
I'll not have you depart once more.
The thought of you has grieved me sore,
Since the first hour I saw you here,
Not knowing the fate, far or near,
For which God had destined you,
Though it was divined, it is true,
As all the court knows now, by rule,
Both by the maiden and the fool,
Struck by Sir Kay the Seneschal.
And you have now confirmed it all,
All that they prophesied about;
Of that none harbours any doubt,
Who, since, of all your chivalry
Has heard the true tale told to me.'
The queen appeared, upon this word,
For she of the whole thing had heard,
Of this knight come from elsewhere;
And when Perceval saw here there,
And he was told that this was she,
And saw the maiden, from whom he
Had won a smile when gazing at her,
He advanced to the encounter,
And said: 'God grant joy and honour
To the noblest, the fairest ever
Of all the ladies that might be,
As all must say who her do see,
And all who her have e'er espied.'
And thus the queen to him replied:
'You are more than welcome here,
As a knight whom it would appear
Has proved of fair and high prowess!'
Then the maid greeted their guest,
She who'd once smiled at Perceval;
She embraced him, and he, withal,

Cried: 'Fair maid, should you have need
Of help, I'll be that knight, indeed
Who'll never fail to bring you aid.'
So she thanked him, the fair maid.

LINES 4579-4693 THE UGLY MAIDEN RAILS AT PERCEVAL'S FAILURE

GREAT joy to the queen and king
Doth Perceval the Welshman bring.
With his lords, doth the king recall
Him to Carlion, and thither go all.
And so by nightfall they returned.
All that night to pleasure they turned,
And so again the whole day through,
Till, on the third day, came in view,
A maiden, riding a dun mule, who
Clasped a whip in her right hand.
Her hair, bound in a double strand,
Was thick and black, and if tis true
What the book says of her, then you
Ne'er so ugly a thing could find,
In Hell itself, while, to my mind,
None has e'er seen iron so black,
Who's been to earth's end and back,
As the colour of her hands and face,
Yet the rest of her, in every place,
Was worse to view, in every way,
For her two eyes, I have to say,
Were holes as small as any rat,
Her nose that of an ape or cat,
Her lips those of an ox or ass.
For yellow egg-yolk might pass,

Her teeth, the colour was so rich,
And she was bearded, like a witch.
Her chest, before, was but a hump,
Behind, her spine a crooked lump,
And her shoulders and her thighs,
Not made for twirling, I'd surmise,
And, below, of stalks like twisted
Willow-wands the legs consisted.
Full fit was she to lead the dance!
Upon her mule she did advance,
Passing slow before each knight,
And ne'er before was such a sight
Seen at a king's court; in the hall,
She hailed the king and barons all,
Except for Perceval alone,
Whom she thus declined to own,
But, mounted on the dun mule's back,
She cried: 'Ah, Perceval, alack,
Fortune's locks are bare behind.
Curse the one that you doth find,
And fails to wish you no good,
For you did not, as you should,
Seize Fortune's locks on sight!
At the Fisher King's, sir knight,
You saw the lance that bleeds pass,
Yet twas so hard for you, alas,
To open your lips and speak
That you thereby failed to seek
The reason why that drop of blood
Fell from the lance of gleaming wood!
And then, of the grail that you saw,
You asked not what noble lord,
What rich man, one served with it.
Unhappy is he whose sky is lit
By perfect weather yet sits dumb,

And waits for better still to come.
And such are you, the sad disgrace,
Who saw it was the time and place
To speak to him, and yet said naught!
In evil hour, a folly you wrought!
In evil hour, you kept silence so,
Whereas, had you sought to know,
The worthy king, who is unsound,
Would have trod upon the ground,
And, healed, held his realm, in peace,
Of which he'll hold nary a piece.
And know you, now, what will arise,
Now the king's denied that prize,
And of his wound is yet unhealed?
Wasteland shall replace the field,
Widowhood be the woman's fate,
Maidens shall prove disconsolate,
And shall as orphans live, for aye,
And many a knight shall sadly die,
And, through you, all shall come to ill.'
Then to the king she turned, at will,
And said: 'King, fret not, I must go,
This night your court I must forego
And find me lodgings far from here.
I know not if you've chanced to hear,
Men speak of the Castle Orgulous,
Well, I must travel to that fortress.
Five hundred and sixty six knights,
That castle holds, all men of might,
And know that there is nary a one
Has not his lady there, every one
Of them noble, courteous and fair.
This I tell you, for none goes there
Without encountering some fight,
A joust, a battle, to delight,

If he'd do deeds of chivalry.
Should he seek them, no lack there'll be.
And he who'd win the greatest prize
In all the world, I can apprise
Of the very place, the strip of ground,
Where such winning might be found,
If any would that venture dare.
On the very top of Montesclaire,
There is a maiden has her seat;
With great honour men would greet
Any man who the siege could raise
Free the maid, and reap the praise.
There would be fame seen and felt;
And the Sword with the Strange Belt
He thus could gird about him, too
If God had granted him so to do.'
Then the maiden's speech ceased,
For she had uttered all she pleased,
And left without another word.

LINES 4694-4787 GAWAIN IS CHALLENGED BY GUINGANBRESIL

GAWAIN when of that maid he heard,
At Montesclaire, rose, with a cry,
Claiming he'd rescue her, or die.
And Girflet, he the son of Do,
Said, God save him, he would go,
And find the Castle Orgulous.
'And I to climb Mount Dolorous,'
Said Kahedin, 'and never rest,
Until I reach its very crest.'
But Perceval spoke otherwise,

Saying while he was yet alive
He'd not lodge two nights together
In one place; nor fail to venture
Through any strange new-heard of pass;
Nor would he fail to surpass,
In battle, any knight who claimed
He was greater than those famed
In fight; nor would he shirk travail,
Until he'd learned, of the grail,
Whom with it was served, and he
The lance that bled again did see,
And to the proven truth was led,
Through being told of why it bled.
Another fifty bold knights there,
Rose to their feet, and did swear,
One to another, gave their word,
That from no fight of which they heard,
Or venture, would they turn away,
Though in some vile land it lay.
And while they spoke of this and more,
Guinganbresil came through the door,
Into the hall, and they made room
For him, when they saw him come.
And he did bear a golden shield,
With a band of azure on its field.
Guinganbresil, who knew the king,
Courteously gave him greeting,
But greeted not Gawain, for he
Accused that lord of treachery,
Calling out: 'Gawain, you slew
My father, and you did so, too,
Without a challenge, to your shame.
Yours be the reproach, and blame,
Thus I accuse you here of treason,
And it is known to every baron

I've uttered not one word untrue.'
At this my Lord Gawain he flew
To his feet, burning with shame,
But Agravain, the Proud by name,
His brother, leapt up, to restrain
Him: 'For the love of God, Gawain,
Bring not shame on your lineage;
From this blame, from this outrage,
The knight seeks to lay upon you,
I will, I promise, here defend you.'
He said: 'My own self, and no other,
Must defend me, my dear brother,
For the defence is mine, you see,
Since he accuses none but me.
Yet if I could but bring to mind
But one misdeed, of any kind,
That I know of against this knight,
I'd make amends, seek peace outright,
And do all, that your friends and mine
Might think right, to make all fine.
Yet what he speaks, tis pure outrage,
I'll prove my honour, see my gage,
Where'er he pleases, here or there.'
He said they'd settle the affair,
Before the King of Escavalon;
Who was, in his opinion,
Far handsomer than Absalom.
'Then,' said Gawain, 'to that kingdom,
I pledge to follow you, sir knight,
And see, there, who is in the right.'
Then Guinganbresil went his way,
While Lord Gawain, without delay,
His preparations did advance.
Then all who had a sound lance,
Or shield, or helm, or fine sword,

Offered it, but he refused, that lord,
To take aught else but was his own.
Seven squires followed him, alone,
And, with each, a mount and shield.
And, now he sought to take the field,
The deepest grief was shown at court;
Torn hair, scarred flesh, faces fraught,
And many a beaten breast remained,
No dame so old but showed her pain,
And, for the knight, revealed her sorrow;
They wept, as there were no tomorrow,
As Lord Gawain went on his way.
Of his adventures, day by day,
Now I shall speak, and you shall hear.

Lines 4788-4860 The tournament at Tintagel

On open ground, he saw appear
A band of knights, at first, and he
Asked of a squire, who willingly
Followed after them and led
A Spanish steed by the head,
The reins held in his right hand
A shield around his neck: 'My man,
Say, who are they who pass by?'
And the squire gave him his reply:
'Sire, it is Meliant de Lis,
A knight known for his bravery.'
'Are you of his household?' 'No, sire,
But of no less a man's,' said the squire,
Droes d'Aves my master's name.'
''T'faith, I know that very same
Droes d'Aves,' said Lord Gawain.

'Whither goes he? Now, tell me plain.'
'Sire, to a tournament he goes,
That Meliant de Lis did propose
Against Tiebaut of Tintagel,
And you should journey there, as well,
And defend it from those without.'
'By God,' said Lord Gawain, 'no doubt;
But was not Meliant de Lis
Raised in Tiebaut's nursery?'
'Yes, God save me, sire, indeed,
His father loved Tiebaut, and he
So trusted in him, as his man,
On his deathbed, he did command
Tiebaut to rear his little son,
And as he asked so it was done,
With care, and as best he could,
Till Meliant, come to true manhood,
Sought the love of Tiebaut's daughter,
And she replied that, if he sought her,
She would ne'er her own troth plight
Till Meliant had become a knight.
He, who desired her passionately,
Had himself made a knight, and he
At once returned, to plead again.
"That shall not be, I now maintain,
I'faith," the maid said, "not until
Before me, you display your skill
In arms, and in the joust do prove,
That you have truly earned my love.
For things we gain at once taste not
As sweet as those that we have got
With pain, nor so agreeably.
Challenge my father to a tourney,
If you would have my love, for I,
Would know without a doubt, or sigh,

That my love was not misplaced,
If twere in you my trust I placed."
So as she wished, Meliant sent
The challenge to a tournament,
For Love it hath such sovereign power,
That all those in Love's sway this hour
Would ne'er deny the least demand,
That Love doth wish, and so command;
And you indeed were good for naught,
If you lent not Tiebaut your support.'
Gawain replied: 'Friend, off you go,
Follow your lord, and stay whole so,
For you have more than had your say!'
Thus the squire went on his way,
And onward Lord Gawain did ride,
Towards Tintagel, for he spied
No other way that he might go.
And Tiebaut both high and low,
Young and old, had gathered in;
His cousins, all his kith and kin,
His neighbours, and every knight,
All there assembled for the fight.

LINES 4861-4918 GAWAIN'S ARRIVAL IS NOTED

BUT there was not a counsellor,
In the town, who advised his lord
To take up arms against his master,
For they feared twould be disaster,
And that he wished their downfall.
So at every gate he raised a wall,
And he closed every entry-way.
The gates were barred, night and day,

Sealed with solid stone and mortar,
And thus no gate required a porter.
Through a postern knights might pass,
Its door indeed not made of glass
But copper, made to last forever,
And this they could open ever,
But forged for it an iron bar,
And set more iron on it by far
Than any modest cart could bear.
And my Lord Gawain came there,
Once he had ceased his journey,
Not to thus attend the tourney
But he must so enter, or return,
There was no other way to turn,
No other road, for seven days.
Finding the postern shut always,
He entered a field below the wall,
Surrounded by a fence, quite tall,
Dismounted, underneath an oak,
And hung his shields up, so the folk,
Within the keep, might see them there;
And more than one felt joy, aware
That the tourney might yet take place.
There was an old lord of their race,
In that castle, who oft did advise,
Being high-born, revered, and wise,
On matters; powerful, rich in land,
Such that, there, not a single man
Failed to trust him, come what may.
Being shown the strangers far away,
Long before they reached the field
And were within the fence revealed,
He went to Tiebaut and declared:
'God save me, sire, but I see there,
Two knights, and more there may be,

Who are of Arthur's company,
And they are making their way here.
Two noblemen might play, tis clear,
A fine part, one could win a tourney,
I think, and do advise, and rightly,
To the tourney you may go hence,
And do so with some confidence,
For you have knights, good ones too,
Fine men-at-arms, and archers who
Each can slay an enemy steed.
And I believe they must indeed
Mass together before the gate.
If pride draws them to their fate,
We it is who shall reap the gain,
And they the loss, and the pain.'

LINES 4919-4986 THE GIRL WITH LITTLE SLEEVES

FOLLOWING the advice he gave,
Tiebaut told the strong and brave
To arm themselves and, henceforth,
Those who wished might issue forth.
Overjoyed were all those knights,
And the squires, quick as they might,
Ran for horses, saddles, armour.
The ladies and the maids of honour
Went to the loftiest place, thereby
To watch the tournament on high;
And saw below them, in the field,
Gawain's baggage train revealed,
And thought, at first, there might be
Seven knights there, in company,
For seven shields they could see,

Hung on the branches of the tree.
Born neath some auspicious star,
That shone upon them from far,
They thought themselves if seven knights
Before their eyes, were set to fight.
Some of the lords thought so too,
But others took a different view:
Saying: 'By God, sire, that knight
Has enough arms and gear he might
Equip a band of seven, and yet
There is none other with him met.
What will he do with seven shields?
No knight was e'er seen in the field
Carrying seven shields together.
For twould be taken for a wonder
If one knight were to bear, I own,
Those seven shields, and all alone.'
Still talking of this strange sight,
The knights issued forth to fight,
While Tiebaut's eldest daughter
Climbed the stairs of the tower;
She'd brought about the tournament;
The younger with her sister went,
Who wore her sleeves so nicely
With such a narrow fit, that she
Was called The Girl with Little Sleeves,
So tight to the arm each did cleave;
And with Tiebaut's two daughters
Went the ladies and maids together
Up to the heights of the tower.
Before the castle, at that hour,
Did the tournament assemble.
And there was none did resemble
Meliant de Lis in handsomeness,
To that his loved one bore witness,

Saying, to all those about her:
'In truth, ladies, I have never,
For, to you, why should I lie,
Seen a knight to please the eye,
As much as Meliant de Lis.
A solace and delight to see
Him is it not; so fine a knight?
For he must sit his mount aright,
And carry well a shield and lance,
Who doth so handsomely advance.'
But her sister, there beside her,
Said there was one handsomer,
And the elder was angered so
She rose to strike the girl a blow.
The ladies sought to detain her
And then to openly restrain her,
From thus attacking her sister,
Though angrier it did her render.

Lines 4987-5058 The ladies pour scorn on Gawain

All to the fight, did now advance,
And the knights broke many a lance,
Dealt many a blow with the sword
And many a brave knight was floored;
And know that dearly did they pay
Who fought with Meliant that day:
None before his lance was found
But he was beaten to the ground;
And if his lance broke, with the blade
Of his sword, wide sweeps he made;
There was no man, far and wide,
Who fought better on either side.

And his beloved knew such joy
She felt obliged to then employ
These words: 'Ladies, here's a wonder,
For you will see his equal never,
Nor hear tell of such a knight!
Behold the best man in a fight
You'll ever see with your two eyes.
He's finer, and his arms he plies
More skilfully, this day, than any.'
Her little sister said: 'I see
A better and a finer man.'
And then the elder one began,
And hot with anger now, was she:
'You, wretch, you've the effrontery
And may it prove your downfall too,
To dare to scorn a creature, you,
Whom I have sought to praise,' cried she.
'Take this then for now, and see
You hold your tongue another time.'
And she slapped her cheek, meantime,
So all her fingers left a mark,
And all the ladies there did hark
To the blow, held and blamed her,
And after spoke again together
Among themselves, of Sir Gawain.
'Dear Lord,' one cried, as if in pain,
'That knight beside the oak-tree there,
Why does he shun this whole affair?'
While one, more junior, was pleased
To claim that he was sworn to peace.
And another spoke then, smilingly:
'Say no more, a merchant is he!'
'A money-changer,' cried a fourth,
'He'll not intend to sally forth,
And hand those poor men who fought

'That knight beside the oak-tree there,
Why does he shun this whole affair?'
Le Morte d'Arthur (1893), Sir Thomas Malory (15th cent) and
Ernest Rhys (1859-1946)
Internet Archive Book Images

All the coins that he has brought.
Don't think I'd tell you all a lie,
There's fine gold and silver, say I
In those trunks, all there on view.'
'Truth, you've an evil tongue on you,'
Cried the little sister, 'you're wrong!
Think you a merchant brought along
That great lance that you see there?
Sure tis my death you deal, I swear,
When such devilish things you say.
By the Holy Spirit to whom I pray,
He seems a knight fit for danger,
No merchant he, or money-changer.
He is a knight it seems to me.'
But the ladies, as one, cried: 'He
Might seem to be, dear sweet friend,
But he is not, and you may depend
On that; he feigns to be a knight
Only because he thinks he might
Escape the tolls by telling lies.
He's a fool, who thinks he's wise,
For, in that crime, he'll be seized,
Charged as a thief, and be pleased,
A wise fool, the gallows to deck,
With a noose tied around his neck.'

LINES 5059-5121 GAWAIN IS TAUNTED BY A SQUIRE

MY Lord Gawain, clearly heard,
All that was spoken, every word,
All that those ladies said of him,
And it shamed and troubled him;
But he thought, and with good reason,

172

'All that those ladies said of him...
shamed and troubled him'
Le Morte d'Arthur (1893), Sir Thomas Malory (15th cent) and
Ernest Rhys (1859-1946)
Internet Archive Book Images

That having been accused of treason
He ought to counter it, as of right;
And if he failed to attend and fight,
According to his pledge, then blame
And dishonour would mar his name,
And those of his line many a year.
And because indeed he went in fear
Of being captured or wounded, he
Kept himself far from the tourney,
Though he longed to join the fray,
For, as he saw, throughout the day
The fight had grown more violent;
While Meliant de Lis had sent
For a stouter lance to do more harm.
All day, until the night brought calm,
The knights fought on before the gate.
Those who'd won, when it grew late,
Stowed the spoils for safe-keeping.
Thus, on across the field, creeping
The ladies saw a squire, who hauled
The stump of a lance; large and bald
He was, and there around his neck
A horse's halter did him bedeck.
One lady called him a fool beside:
'God save me, sir squire,' she cried,
'You must be an idiot, twice found,
To search about there, on the ground,
For battered halters, and lance-tips,
Broken standards, and bridle-bits,
And yet still call yourself a squire.
Raise your sights if you would aspire;
He lowers himself, who aims low,
And here I see, in that field below,
Not far from you, I would surmise,
Many an undefended prize.

He's a fool who thinks not on it
When he's well-nigh standing on it!
And then, the most courteous knight
Ever born, stands by, you might
Pluck his moustache, he'd not stir.
Don't go for paltry spoils, dear sir!
All those horses, and all the rest,
Take for me, if with sense you're blessed,
For no one will dispute your claim.'
Over the field the squire now came,
To one of the mounts he gave a blow
With his lance-butt, and cried: 'Ho!
Vassal, are you in a parlous state
That you stand here all day and wait,
And of the fight will not partake,
To pierce a shield, or lance break?'
'Why is it your concern?' said he.
'Be on your way, fly far from me;
The reason why I thus remain,
May, one day, to you show plain,
But, by my life, tis not this day,
I'd deign my reason to display.
Go now, be about your business.'

Lines 5122-5173 Gawain lodges with Garin, son of Bertain

So the squire fled him, more or less;
Nor were there any more did seek,
Of aught that angered him, to speak.
The tournament lasted little longer,
Many knights were taken prisoner,
And many a steed had been slain;

The townsfolk most spoils did gain,
Though the attackers took the prize,
And, on parting, they both devised
A meeting on the morrow, to fight
Throughout the day, until the night.
So they departed, and all those men
Come from the castle returned again,
And entered through the postern gate.
And my Lord Gawain was straight
Upon the heels of those who entered,
And he, before the gate, encountered
That aged lord, the wise councillor,
Who had, that day, advised his lord
To then commence the tournament,
And now, with courteous intent,
Asked Gawain to lodge with him,
For, graciously, he spoke to him:
'All is ready in the castle, sire,
All that you need or might desire;
Your lodgings are prepared for you.'
Lodge here with us, for should you
Take to the road, and go your way,
You'll find no place nearby to stay.
Thus I'd beseech you to remain.'
'Thanks be to you,' said Lord Gawain,
'Sire, I will, you shall be obeyed,
For worse offers have I heard made.'
The lord led him to his lodging,
And while, of this and that, speaking,
He asked him why, upon that day,
He'd not borne arms amidst the fray,
And why Gawain had but stood by.
And he told him all the reason why:
That he had been accused of treason,
Dare not be wounded, for that reason,

Nor could he suffer to be detained
Until he had his honour regained,
Free of the shame that on him lay.
If he failed to appear, on the day
Appointed, he and his every friend
Would be dishonoured; to that end
He had thus refrained from the fight.
The lord greatly praised the knight,
Greeting his speech, with satisfaction;
That he'd refrained from the action
Of the tourney, seemed only right.
Into his courtyard he led the knight,
And they dismounted, and entered.

LINES 5174-5257 THE ELDER SISTER CONSPIRES AGAINST GAWAIN

BUT the folk, in the town, dissented,
And, gathering to denounce Gawain,
Said that their lord should him arraign,
And that he should arrest him straight.
And his eldest daughter, who did hate
The younger sister so, worked away
Against them both, as best she may:
'Sire, said she, 'I think you are none
The worse for this day, but have won
More than you think you have and I
Will gladly tell you the reason why.
You need do no more than simply
Command that your men go swiftly
And take that knight, whom not one
Will defend, and defence he's none,
For he lives by his deceit and guile.

Into this town he brings, the while,
Shields, and lances, and warhorses,
And he leads about those coursers
Exempt from tolls, he, in the guise
Of a knight; they, not merchandise.
Now grant him his deserts, that one.
He lodges with Garin, Bertain's son,
Who in his house has let him stay,
For he entered it this very day,
I saw his host lead him inside.'
And thus the elder sister vied
To bring upon him every shame.
And her father pursued the same
End, indeed, for he sought to go
Straight to the house, where we know
Gawain was lodged, the very door.
And when his younger daughter saw
Him departing in such a manner,
She slipped out the rear, by another
Way, taking care none should see her,
And running quickly was, soon after,
Before the door where lodged Gawain,
The house of Garin, son of Bertain,
Who had two daughters, also fair.
And, when the girls found here there,
And saw it was their own sweet lady,
Joy was theirs, unreservedly,
An honest joy, you'll understand.
Then each took her by the hand,
And, joyfully, led her inside,
On lips and eyes their kisses plied.
Meanwhile Garin had remounted,
He was among the wealthy counted;
And, at his side, his son Herman,
And set out for the court, his plan,

Being that they, when thus abroad,
Would, there, confer with their lord.
Instead, they met him in the street.
And their lord his vassals did greet,
And they asked him whither he rode,
And he replied: why, to their abode,
As he desired some entertainment.
'Why, there's no grief in that intent
Nor any annoy,' Garin replied,
'You'll see, for there he doth abide,
The finest knight to ride the earth.'
'Tis not to see him, not for mirth,
I come, I'faith, but for his arrest.
He's but a merchant is your guest,
Selling horses, for he's no knight.'
'What, sire! And have I heard aright?
Cried Garin, 'dire words you afford
Me; I'm your man and you my lord,
Yet, as for myself, and my lineage,
I'll withdraw from you all homage;
And all shall defy you, from today,
Rather than suffer you, this way,
To bring dishonour on my lodging.'
'God save me, sir, for no such thing
Do I intend there,' much distressed,
His lord replied, 'nor house nor guest,
Aught but honour will have from me,
Tis only that, by my faith, you see,
I have received the firmest warning
Against such deceits, this morning.'
'All thanks then,' cried the vavasor,
'And it would be the greatest honour
To have you come, and meet my guest.

LINES 5258-5329 THE YOUNGER SISTER COMPLAINS TO GAWAIN

SIDE by side they now progressed,
At once, towards Gawain's lodging,
And the vassal his lord did bring
To his house, where my Lord Gawain
Rested; and when he saw them plain,
Ever courteous, as they drew near,
He rose, and cried: 'Be welcome here!'
The two, in turn, both greeted him,
And then they sat down beside him.
The lord of the land then inquired
Of Sir Gawain why it transpired,
That he chose not to fight that day,
But from the tourney turned away.
And Gawain, being not annoyed,
The power of truth then employed,
Saying twas neither sin nor shame,
But having been accused, by name,
Of treason by a certain knight,
He went to the king's court to fight,
And so defend himself from the claim.
'You had good reason for the same,
Tis fair excuse,' the lord replied.
'Where is this court that shall decide?
Sire, said he, I must journey on
To seek the King of Escavalon;
And must go at once, so I believe.'
'You'll be escorted when you leave,'
Said the lord, 'to that place you seek.
And since through lands poor and bleak

You must pass to journey there,
I'll give you pack-horses to bear
Provisions for you on the ride.'
And my Lord Gawain replied
He would not, for it would avail
If he could but find food for sale;
He might have ample nourishment
And horses too, where'er he went,
Thus would he find all he needed;
He asked for naught. Twas conceded,
And the lord rose to take his leave;
As he went to go, he did perceive
His younger daughter, who now ran
To clasp her arms about the man,
Or at least she embraced the leg
Of Lord Gawain, and thus did beg:
'Sire, please, I've come here to you
To complain about my sister, who
Slapped me hard; grant me justice.'
Gawain said not a word to this,
Unsure as to whom it was said,
But set his hand upon her head;
And the girl tugged at him again:
'To you, fair sire, I thus complain,
About my sister, whom I do not
Hold dear or love, such is my lot;
She shamed me on account of you.'
'And why is that my affair too?
What redress for you, can I win?'
Her father, hearing her, came in
Again, and at once demanded
Of her: 'Daughter, who commanded
That you complain to this knight?'
But Gawain said: 'Sire, I might
Rather say that, although, to me,

She spoke somewhat childishly,
And girlishly, I'll not refuse;
Tomorrow, for a while, I choose
Instead to be her knight, indeed.'
'Thanks be to you, fair sire,' said she,
And such was her joy, now complete,
She bowed down to his very feet.
Then they left without more ado.

LINES 5330-5420 A SLEEVE IS PREPARED AS A TOKEN

NOW Tiebaut set his daughter too
Upon his palfrey and, this done,
Asked how the quarrel had begun,
As they both rode back together.
And she told him all, whatever
Was the truth, from end to end:
'Sire, it was my sister's fault,
Who declared, ere her assault,
That Meliant de Lis was best
Of all the knights, and handsomest.
And I looked down and there below
In the field was that knight, and so,
I could not keep from telling her
That, on the contrary, down there
One fairer than him could be seen.
And, for that true thing, I have been
Called a wretch, and slapped hard, there.
And cursed be all who think that fair!
I'd let my braids both be sheared
Right to my nape, if it appeared,
(Though quite hideous I would be
If they were to do all that to me),

182

That tomorrow at the tourney
That knight, amidst the melee,
Might do for Meliant de Lis;
And then all the cries would cease,
My sister utters, blown away.
For she so lauded him this day,
That all the ladies were in pain;
Yet a great wind dies, with a little rain!'
The lord said: 'Daughter, I decree
That a token, to him, in courtesy,
You shall send; a sleeve, maybe.'
She answered, in her naivety:
'Willingly, if you tell me so,
But my sleeves they are so narrow,
I wouldn't dare to send him one.
Twere worse than to send him none,
For he'd value it not a whit.'
'Dear daughter, let me think on it,'
Said her father, 'now say naught
For such, readily, may be sought.'
And so conversing, clasping her
In his arms, he bore her further,
And found solace in her the more;
Thus they came to the palace door.
When the elder sister saw her,
Saw how he embraced her sister,
She was angered to the very heart:
'Whence is she, sire, from what part
Comes The Girl with the Little Sleeves?
She knows such ruses, and deceives,
A host of tricks she's quickly learned.
Whence are you and she returned?'
'And you,' he said, 'what's it to you?
You'd best say naught; give her, her due,
Far better than you doth she behave,

Who pull her tresses, at her do rave,
And slap her face, which angers me.
You show the girl scant courtesy.'
Then was she much discomfited,
At all that her father had said,
And his scorn, quite taken aback.
Of crimson samite he'd no lack;
The cloth was drawn from a coffer,
And he had made, for his daughter,
A sleeve: twas both long and wide.
Calling his youngest to his side,
He said: 'Now, daughter, in the morn,
You must make your way, at dawn,
To the knight, ere he choose to go.
Give him this sleeve, for love, so
He will bear it in the tournament,
Since to tourney he doth consent.'
And, to her father, she replied,
That as soon as e'er she spied
The dawn of day she would rise
And dress herself in fair guise.
At this, her father went his way,
While she most joyfully did say
To her companions, they must not
Let her sleep too long, but what,
In the morning, they must do
Was wake her, and quickly too,
If they sought her love; outright,
At the first glow of morning light.
And they replied that, willingly,
As soon as ever they should see
The light of morn, at daybreak,
They'd ensure she was awake.

Lines 5421-5501 Gawain defeats Meliant de Lis

THE girl woke at the break of day,
And, all alone, she made her way
To the lodgings in which had lain
Her champion, but Lord Gawain
Had already risen with the dawn,
And had gone to church that morn,
To hear the mass celebrated;
And so the demoiselle waited,
At Garin's house, while he prayed.
And many a fine prayer was made,
With many a chant, high and clear,
While he heard whate'er was to hear.
But when from church he came again
She rose to her feet, before Gawain,
Did the girl, and cried: 'God save you,
And joy in today's joust, grant you!
And bear this sleeve, for love for me.'
'Thank you, my friend, and willingly,'
My Lord Gawain now answered her.
Not long after the knights did gather,
To arm themselves, and one and all
They massed outside the castle wall,
And every lady, and every maiden,
Climbed to the high towers again,
To the windows, to view the sights,
And watch the assembly of the knights,
For proud and strong they seemed to be.
Before all, rode Meliant de Lis,
Charging ahead so swiftly, mind,
At least a hundred yards behind

Him, the rest the ground did cover.
The elder daughter, his fond lover,
Watched, and could not hold her tongue,
Crying: 'Ladies, now see him come,
The knight who is of chivalry
The flower, and holds sovereignty.'
Now, my Lord Gawain did follow
And fast as his charger would go,
Met Meliant, who showed no fear,
But on Gawain his lance did sheer,
While Gawain dealt him such a blow
And brought Meliant such pain and woe,
That he fell to the ground, unmanned;
While Gawain took the steed in hand,
Seized the reins, and calling a squire,
Told him to go, twas his desire,
Take it to her, for whom he fought,
And say it was from him, in short;
That the first spoils he had won,
This day, he wished her to own.
And the squire the saddled steed
To the maiden did swiftly lead,
Who had watched there below,
Seated there at the high window,
The fall of proud Meliant de Lis.
And cried: 'Sister, now you see,
Meliant de Lis, now fallen, lies,
Whom you so praised to the skies.
Well you know to whom praise is due!
What I said yesterday's proven true,
God save me, for everyone can see
There is a better knight than he!'
Thus she taunted her sister bent
On riling her, twas her intent,
Till the elder was badly stung,

And cried aloud: 'Wretch, hold your tongue!
If I hear another word from you
I'll give you such a slap, or two,
You'll not see to stand upright.'
'O sister, the Lord keep in sight,'
Said the little maid to the other,
'For since twas truth I did discover
You ought not to slap me so.
I'faith, I saw him take that blow,
And so did you, as clear as I.
It seems to me that he must lie
Still awhile, till he's fit to rise.
Though you burst before my eyes,
I'll tell the truth, and tell it all,
No lady here but saw him fall,
Head over heels, and then lie flat!'

Lines 5502-5599 Gawain takes courteous leave of all

She'd have dealt her a blow for that,
If she'd been allowed to act so,
But those ladies barred the blow,
Who beside the two were sitting.
And then they saw a squire coming,
Who led a horse in his right hand.
He found the girl there, as planned,
And presented her with the steed,
She thanked him sixty times indeed,
And he went to convey her thanks
To Lord Gawain, amidst the ranks
Of knights who'd escaped disaster,
Of whom he seemed lord and master,
For there was nary a knight he met

Who his lance did soon forget;
For their stirrups he left empty.
Never before so intent had he
Seemed on winning every mount.
Four steeds it was, at the last count,
That he gained with his right hand.
He sent the first, you understand,
To the little maid; then to delight
His host's wife, whom the knight
Thus pleased indeed, he sent one;
A third her eldest daughter won;
Her other daughter had the fourth.
And he returned as he'd gone forth,
When all was ended, with the spoils,
My Lord Gawain; for all his toils,
All the honours his, on that day.
Now it had not yet reached midday
When Gawain left off the tourney,
And, as he left, there were so many
Knights with him, so vast a suite
About him, that they filled the street
And all he met did then enquire,
To know of him, their sole desire,
Whom he was, and of what country.
And the little maid ran directly
To meet him there at Garin's door,
And the first thing she did, before
All else, was to grasp his stirrup tight,
Then she gave greeting to her knight,
Saying: 'A thousand thanks, fair sire!'
And he knew well all her desire,
So he answered her, gallantly:
'Age will snow white hairs on me,
My dear, ere I cease to serve you,
Where'er I go and, far from you

Though I be, twill ne'er be so far,
That, if you need me where you are,
And I know, aught can prevent me
Being there; send, and there I'll be.'
'A thousand thanks, sire,' said she.
Thus were they talking, she and he,
When her father came, and again
And again, did beg of Lord Gawain,
That he remain with them that night,
As their honoured guest, as was right.
However, my Lord Gawain declined
To remain, he said that, to his mind,
It could not be, then in nigh the same
Breath, his host asked him his name.
'Sire, Gawain am I called, and I
Have never concealed it when I
Was asked my name in any place,
Nor have I, before any man's face,
Spoken it, ere twas asked of me.'
When his host understood that he
Had as his guest my Lord Gawain,
His heart was filled with joy, amain,
And he cried: 'Sire, stay with me,
Partake of our hospitality,
For one more night, for I have not
Served you nigh on enough in aught;
And, never in all my life, I swear,
Have I seen a knight anywhere,
To whom I'd rather do honour.'
But though he would keep him longer,
My Lord Gawain denied his pleas.
And the little maid, she did seize
Him by the foot and gave it a kiss;
Nor ill nor foolish was she in this;
And him to God she did commend.

And my Lord Gawain did attend
To her, and asked the reason,
And she replied to his question,
That when she bestowed the kiss
On his foot, her intent was this:
That he would remember her so
In every place that he might go.
And he said: 'Doubt me not, dear friend,
For, if God aids me, you may depend
On this: that I'll forget you never,
Nor be far distant from you ever.'
Then he took his leave of his host,
And the rest, but of him the most,
Commending to God one and all.

LINES 5600-5721 GAWAIN ENTERS
THE CASTLE OF ESCAVALON

NOW, that night it did so befall
Gawain lodged at an abbey grange;
All he needed they did arrange.
And early the next morning he
Rode out again on his journey;
And he came across a herd of deer,
Grazing as they went, quite near
To the plain, on the forest border.
He thus gave Yvonet the order,
Who one of his mounts did lead,
The best of all of them, indeed,
And bore a lance, stout and strong,
To halt; and bring the lance along,
And see the saddle girth was tight
On the horse, there, on his right.

Swiftly the squire did then advance,
And handed him his shield and lance.
On that mount, he chased the deer,
And twisted and turned, full near,
Until, beside a thorn, he caught
A white doe, of those he sought.
Across its neck he laid his lance,
Seeking to check its swift advance;
But the white doe, leaping aside,
After the other deer did glide.
He pressed so hard that he'd almost
Have caught her now, he was so close,
If his charger had not cast a shoe.
Finding the doe now lost to view,
He had Yvonet dismount swiftly,
For the steed was hobbling badly,
The squire did as his lord decreed
Raised its leg, and found indeed
The horse had lost a shoe, and said:
'Sire he must be re-shod; instead
Of the chase, we must wander on,
Until some place we come upon
Where a farrier may re-shoe him.'
Thus they wandered on, at whim,
Until they spied a hunting party
Ride from a castle, at the ready,
Before them boys, with clothes girt,
Who took to the road with a spurt,
Next lads on foot who led the hounds,
Huntsmen racing o'er the ground,
Each with his sharp hunting-spear.
Behind these archers did appear,
Carrying their quivers and bows,
And next the knights in hunting clothes.
And after every other knight,

Two more, on chargers, hove in sight,
One a youth who, beside the rest,
Appeared by far the handsomest.
He alone greeted my Lord Gawain,
Took him by the hand, to detain
Him, saying: 'Sire, I beg of you
Follow the road, that is in view,
Dismount at my house, for reason
Cries out, tis the day and season,
You're destined to lodge with us.
I have a sister, most courteous,
Who'll welcome you with delight;
Thither he'll lead you, the knight
You see here, who rides beside me.
Go my dear companion,' said he,
'Go, for I send you, and no other,
To lead him there, to my sister.
First give her greeting, and then say
That I do command her, this day,
By all the love and loyalty
That should exist twixt her and me,
That if she e'er has loved a knight
She shall love this lord, at first sight,
And hold him dear, in no other
Way than she doth me, her brother.
Such solace and such company
She must provide, and so please
Our guest, until we may return.
While she doth graciously concern
Herself with him, return to me,
And ride as swiftly as can be,
Then, when the moment offers, we
Will home, to keep him company.'
The knight turned his horse's head,
And Lord Gawain to the castle led,

Escavalon, where twas his fate
To be viewed with a mortal hate.
Yet there his face was still unknown,
None had e'er seen him yet, I own,
So, he entered in unguardedly.
It sat above an arm of the sea,
And Lord Gawain gazed and saw
It walls and keep, both strong and sure,
So that the place feared no attack.
He looked about, and saw no lack;
Twas peopled, with fine folk all,
And every moneychanger's stall
Was heaped with silver and gold.
He saw streets and squares unfold
Full of those who worked away
At diverse trades, so on that day
The trade itself was most diverse.
One his helm-making did rehearse,
Others chain-mail, lances, shields,
That bridles; spurs this one yields;
He sharpens, he polishes blades.
Some fulled cloth, others displayed
The weaving, combing, and shearing,
Others, in gold and silver working,
Made many fine and lovely things,
There were belt-buckles and rings,
Enamelled jewellery; every kind
Of dish or goblet, you could find.
You might as well think and say
That every day was market day,
So full of merchandise that town,
Marvelling, they rode up and down;
Such beeswax, pepper, spices there,
Such cloth, grey or lined with vair,
And every other kind of ware.

They rode along, and lingered where
They wished, till the keep was at hand.
There squires ran to take command
Of their steeds, and all else they owned.

LINES 5722-5765 GAWAIN MEETS THE FAIR MAID OF ESCAVALON

THE knight entered the keep alone
Except indeed for my Lord Gawain,
And, clasping his right hand again,
He led him to the sister's chamber,
And said: 'Fair friend, your brother
Sends you his greeting, and requests
Concerning this knight, his guest,
That you honour and serve him truly.
And asks that you do so willingly;
Not grudge him aught, nor keep apart,
But do so with as good a heart
As if you were his only sister,
As if he were your only brother.
And take care not to seem averse
To his wishes, instead rehearse
Generosity, and loving-kindness;
Be gracious, in all your address.
I must return now to the woods;
Think on this.' She said she would.
'For blessed be he who sends to me
Such company as this shall be!
Who sends such a one as this,
Hates me not, all thanks be his.
Fair sire, you'll sit here you see,'
Said the maid, 'here, beside me.

My brother, and your nobility,
Demand I bear you company.'
The messenger now turned away,
Who might, indeed, no longer stay;
While my lord did there remain,
Having small reason to complain,
Being alone with a maid, sitting
Beside one both fair and charming,
So self-possessed that, all in all,
She thought there no harm at all
In finding herself alone with him.
Of love he spoke, and she to him,
For blind folly it would have been
To talk there of aught else, I ween.
My Lord Gawain did make request
That she love him, as for the rest,
He swore that he'd be hers forever;
And she refused him not, but rather
Granted her love most willingly.

LINES 5766-5819 GAWAIN IS ACCUSED AND THE MAID DENOUNCED

YET a vassal entered, suddenly,
Who knew of my Lord Gawain;
Much to their great hurt and pain,
As they merely exchanged a kiss,
Though they had great joy of this.
And, unable to hold his tongue,
Shouted, at the top of his lungs,
In a noisy display of virtue:
'Woman, now shame be on you!
Be, at God's hand, to ruin hurled,

For the one man in all the world,
You should hate above all others
You'd clasp, as if you were lovers,
Have him embrace you, and kiss!
Woman, wretched, ever foolish,
You should do now what you ought,
Tear the heart from him, in short,
Rather than kiss him on the lip.
For though your kisses might grip
His heart thus, and draw it thence,
Yet it were better to tear it hence,
With your two hands from out his breast;
For thus you ought, as I attest,
If as a woman you'd act rightly.
Yet no woman does such, for she
Who hates evil and loves the good
Tis wrong to call woman, none should;
For she who only loves that same,
She forfeits her right to that name.
But woman you are, so much is true;
That man, who sits beside you, slew
Your father, yet you kiss and tease.
When women can do as they please,
They care naught for the rest, tis plain.'
With this, and before Lord Gawain
Could say a word, he sprang away,
The maid fell to the floor, and lay
A long while there, in a faint still,
Upon the stone flags, there, until
My Lord Gawain had revived her.
And when to her feet he'd raised her,
Pale and wan, with fear she sighed,
And once she could breathe, she cried:
'Ah, now we both shall meet our death!
We both shall breathe our last breath;

I'll die for love of you, yet wrongly,
And you, I think, will die for me.
Soon the folk of this town will come,
Ten thousand, to pronounce our doom,
And before the tower they will mass.
And yet, ere that may come to pass,
I'll arm you; there are weapons here.
One brave man could hold, tis clear,
This tower, against a mighty army.'

Lines 5820-5868 Guinganbresil reaches Escavalon

So she ran, and brought them swiftly,
And then she clad my Lord Gawain,
Who did not arm himself in vain,
Rather he laid many a man low;
To hold the door against the foe,
None could be summoned fine as he.
Now not one word of this did he
Who'd offered him lodging know;
He was returning swiftly though,
From the chase, where he hunted,
While all the townsfolk assaulted
The keep with their steel picks still.
And twas now that Guinganbresil,
Through unforeseen coincidence,
Came riding to the castle entrance,
And found himself all dumbfounded
At the way the wretches pounded
Against the tower, for naught he knew
Of my Lord Gawain's entering too.
But once he had discovered all,
He forbade them, whate'er befall,

From displaying such temerity,
Bold though they seemed to be,
As to seek to dislodge a stone,
Or a life they'd no longer own.
Yet they cried they cared naught
For him, no, beware; they sought
To bring it down upon his head,
If he sided with Gawain instead.
And when he saw that his threat
Was all in vain, he thought to let
The folk alone, and seek the king,
And confront him with this thing,
This riot, amongst the populace.
The king, returning from the chase,
He met, and told him of the same:
'Sire they bring on you great shame,
This mayor, and all the aldermen,
Who since morn, time and again,
Have assailed your tower. If you
Act not, if no charges ensue,
Then I shall hold you in ill favour.
I have attacked Gawain's honour,
Charged him with treason, as you know,
And yet you've chosen to bestow
Your hospitality on that knight;
Thus tis but reasonable and right
That, if you ope to him your hall,
Shame nor hurt shall on him fall.'

LINES 5869-5926 IT IS PROPOSED THAT GAWAIN SEEK THE LANCE THAT BLEEDS

SAID the king, to Guinganbresil:
'My Lord, once we are there he will
Know none, from that very instant.
What is occurring at this moment
Surprises, troubles me indeed,
But I cannot wonder they exceed
All bounds, for they do hate him so.
Yet from prison I'll keep him though,
And from all harm, if I but can.
For since I have lodged the man,
I shall treat him with great honour.'
Thus, they approached the tower,
A great noise the crowd did make;
There he told the mayor to take
The people with him, and to go;
And since the mayor wished it so,
All vanished, to the very last man.
In the castle, dwelt a gentleman,
Who was a native of that town,
And counselled all the country round,
For his wisdom was great indeed.
'Sire,' he said, 'now you have need
Of a sound and loyal counsellor.
Surely none here should wonder,
Since he committed treachery
Against your father that day he
Slew him, that they, hating him
With a mortal hate, assailed him;
Tis due cause, as you well know.

Now he's an honoured guest, though,
You should ensure, and guarantee,
He's not killed here, and goes free.
And then, with no word of a lie,
Guinganbresil, whom here I spy,
Who charged him with treachery
At Arthur's court, that guarantee
Should also give, and protection.
Now all that is clear, the action
I propose, is that since he came
To your court to clear his name,
He should be offered a respite,
And that he should seek, this knight,
The lance whose iron tip drips blood,
Being such that a fresh drop would
Ever be there, were it wiped clean.
He may go, and the lance be seen,
Or may choose to stay, in prison,
And thus grant you a better reason
For holding him in your duress,
Than you now rightly do possess;
Such the punishment I do name.
For there's no prison you could name
None so oppressive, I am sure
He could not, endlessly, endure.
One should burden one's enemy
With the hardest task one can see;
No better task can I now offer
To ensure the man doth suffer.'

LINES 5927-6008 GAWAIN SETS OUT TO SEEK THE LANCE

To this the king gave his consent,
And to his sister's room he went
Where he found her much aggrieved,
She stood, and his greeting received,
As did Lord Gawain, who appeared
Unmoved, there being naught he feared;
He neither shook, nor changed colour.
Guinganbresil advanced, and offered
Some idle words, as do the vain:
'My Lord Gawain, my Lord Gawain,
I granted you protection, true,
But, you'll recall, I said to you,
That you were not, being overbold,
To enter towns my lord doth hold,
Nor yet this castle, unless, I say,
You found there was no other way.
So you have no reason to complain
Of aught here that brings you pain.'
Then the wise counsellor, said he:
'God save me, sire, all that must be
Set aside, for what reparation
Could he seek for aggravation
By such as these, toward such a one?
Why the case itself would run,
Till the Day of Judgement were here!
The matter stands thus, it doth appear:
My lord the king, he hath this day
Commanded me that I should say,
So long as you and Gawain agree,
That a brief respite there should be,

To the matter for a year and a day,
While my Lord Gawain take his way
And seek the lance whose iron tip
Drips blood, and ever it doth drip
Though the blood be wiped away;
And tis written that on a day
All the wide realm of Logres,
Which was once a land of ogres,
Will be destroyed by that lance.
My lord would have you advance
Your oath and pledge, and so swear.'
'Then, indeed, I would much prefer,'
Said Lord Gawain, 'to linger here
And languish thus for seven years,
Or die, than that I e'er should take
An oath I might be forced to break.
I am not so afeared of death
That I'd not rather save my breath,
And thus endure my death unsworn,
Than live in shame, and be forsworn.'
'Fair sire,' cried the gentleman,
'Twill bring dishonour to no man,
I'faith, twill be no more than to
Swear now, as I would have you do,
That you will seize every chance,
Within your power, to seek the lance.
But if the lance you fail to find,
Nor can return, then, to my mind,
You will be quit of this your vow.'
'That,' said he, 'I'll swear to now,
Subject to all that you have said.'
So the gentleman commanded
A precious reliquary be sought,
And then, once it had been brought,
Gawain swore indeed he would

Seek out the lance that dripped with blood,
Thus a year and a day's respite
Was granted, ere there be a fight
Twixt him, and Guinganbresil;
And Gawain escaped from peril.
He now took leave of the maid,
And to his squires he relayed
The news that they must turn again
For home and leave their lord, Gawain,
With but one mount, his Gringalet.
And, weeping now, they turned away
From their lord, and they were gone.
More of such grief to dwell upon,
And all their tears, displeases me,
While of Lord Gawain, the story
Speaks no more; so now I shall
Take up the tale of Perceval.

LINES 6009-6090 PERCEVAL IS ADMONISHED FOR HIS IRRELIGION

PERCEVAL, so says the story,
Had, long since, lost his memory,
And of God he thought no longer.
Five Aprils, and five Mays later,
Five years he'd spent passing by
Church and chapel that met his eye,
Yet entering not, nor one prayer
To God or his saints offering there;
Five years whose days he sought still,
With deeds of chivalry to fill,
With all kinds of strange adventures,
Hardships, and perilous ventures;

Thus he journeyed, finding those
Most testing, for such he chose,
And with naught did he contend
He could not conquer, in the end.
Sixty knights, of worth, he fought,
And sent them to King Arthur's court,
In those five years of battle dire.
Thus did he spend five years entire
And all without a thought of God.
Five years later his charger trod
Through a tract of wilderness;
Armed completely, nonetheless,
As was his wont, he rode that day,
And met three knights upon the way;
With them ten ladies who, he found,
Went bare-footed, in woollen gowns,
And, also, their heads were hidden
By their hoods, as they were bidden.
That he was armed from head to toe,
And with his shield and lance did go,
Amazed them, for to save their souls
These ladies, as if they trod hot coals,
Their penitence bare-foot did make,
For all their sins, and the Lord's sake.
And, of the knights, one of the three
Called to Perceval: 'Tarry, by me!
Believe you not in Christ the Lord,
Who to us the New Law did accord,
And gave this law to Christian folk?
There is no good reason to cloak
Yourself in armour, in full pride,
On the day that Jesus Christ died.'
And Perceval who'd not a thought
Given to hour or day, or aught
Of this, troubled at heart, replied.

'What day then is today?' he cried.
'What day, sire? Do you not know?
Tis Good Friday, when we all go
Honouring the cross and, within
Our hearts, do bewail our sins.
He hung upon the cross this day,
For thirty pieces, they did betray
Him, who of every sin is free.
For all the world's sins did He
Become a man, the sins that we
Are marred by, God and man in one,
And of the Virgin born, a son
Of the Holy Spirit conceived,
When God flesh and blood received,
Such that His true divinity
In human form this earth did see.
Who holds this not to be the case,
Shall never look upon His face.
He was born of the Virgin, and
Took on the soul and form of man,
In holiest divinity.
Upon this day, I say to thee,
He hung upon the cross, indeed,
And from Hell his friends He freed.
This day is holy, for Our Lord
Both saved the living, and restored
The dead to their new life again.
He saved us all, despite his pain;
He triumphed over sin and hate,
Gracing our pitiful estate;
For, when raised upon the cross,
He raised us all from pain and loss.
All who hold Him in reverence
Should spend this day in penitence.'

LINES 6091-6151 PERCEVAL MEETS THE HERMIT

'FROM whence now come you, then?'
Said Perceval. 'From the best of men,
A holy hermit, both good and wise;
In the forest his dwelling lies.
So holy that he lives, I own,
By the grace of God alone.'
'And, in God's name, what sought you there?
What did you do? How did you fare?'
'Why, sir,' one of the ladies said,
'We of the sins we've committed
Made confession, did counsel ask;
Performing thus the greatest task
We Christians can, who, restored,
Would be pleasing to Our Lord.'
All that Perceval heard did so
Soften him, and pleased him so,
He wished to talk with that good man.
'I'd go there, swiftly as I can,
To that holy hermit, today,
If I but knew the nearest way.'
'Sire, who would reach that place
Must go the path you now face,
And note all the branches, dotted
Here and there, that we knotted,
With our hands, along the way,
That none here might go astray;
We twisted them in that manner.
So they'd find the hermit's shelter.'
To God, each other commending,
Their questions now had ending;

And Perceval entered on his road;
Venting heartfelt sighs, he rode;
Sins, of which he now repented,
Toward God, he thus lamented.
Beneath the trees, as his tears fell,
He rode and, at the hermit's cell,
Dismounted and disarmed, then he
Tied his steed to a hornbeam tree.
Next, he entered the chapel there,
A little room, where, at prayer,
He found the hermit and a priest,
And an acolyte, he not the least
Of them, beginning the service,
The noblest that in holy place is
Spoken, and indeed the sweetest.
Perceval, like one who confessed,
Fell to his knees on entering,
And the hermit summoned him,
Seeing his sad humility,
The teardrops falling ceaselessly,
And running swiftly down his face.
Perceval, feeling deep disgrace,
At having sinned against the Lord,
Seizing him by the foot, implored
Him to counsel him in God's name,
Hands clasped, bowed low in shame,
Since great need of counsel had he.
And the saintly man said, sweetly,
That he should make confession,
Of his sins, for their remission
Confession and repentance won.

Lines 6152-6222 He speaks of the grail, and Perceval's genealogy

'OH, sir, for five years past, I'm one,
Who's known not what he was doing,
Not loving God, nor believing
In Him, nor doing aught but ill.'
'Ah, dear friend, pray that still
He may have mercy on the soul
Of His sinner; your tale unfold,
Of the manner of your sinning.'
'Oh sir, beside the Fisher King,
Upon a time, I saw the lance,
That drips blood as it doth advance,
While, of the grail, that I observed,
I know not whom, by it, was served.
Since then I've been so sorely tried,
I've wished indeed that I had died.
And then, I did forget Our Lord,
Not once his mercy I implored,
Nor did one deed that, to me,
Deserves mercy from such as He.'
'Ah, dear friend,' the hermit said,
'How are you named, where bred?'
'Perceval am I,' he replied.
At the name, the hermit sighed,
For that name the hermit knew.
'Brother,' he said, 'harm came to you,
Through a sin you knew not, brother.
Twas the grief you caused your mother,
On that day when you left her side,
And from that grief it was she died,

For she fell, swooning, as you saw,
At the bridgehead, beside her door.
Because of the sin you thus incurred,
You failed to ask, said not a word,
About the lance, or of the grail;
Thus the ill that plagues your tale.
And know, you'd not have endured,
If you mother had not implored
God to keep you in his care.
So powerful her parting prayer,
That God has protected you
From death, and from prison too.
You sinned when silence seized your tongue,
When you saw the drop that sprung
From the lance that passed you by,
And never asked the reason why.
The fool, who asked not, of the grail,
Whom, by it, one serves, did fail.
Whom one serves by it, is my brother;
And our sister was your mother.
And then is the rich Fisher King
Son to him of whom I'm speaking,
Who has himself served by the grail.
And think not that from that grail
Lamprey, salmon, or pike has he;
A single host, assuredly,
That in the grail one brings to him,
Sustains and warms the life in him.
So holy a thing is the grail,
And he, so spiritual, without fail
The host within the grail, no more,
Maintains his life, so it endure.
For twelve whole years, that chamber
He's sought not once to leave, ever,
There, where the grail did enter in.

Now absolution for your sin
I wish to grant, ere you depart.'
'Dear uncle, with all my heart,
I'd welcome it. And as my mother
Was your sister, you ought rather
To call me nephew and I, therefore,
You uncle, and love you the more.'

LINES 6223-6292 THE HERMIT, HIS UNCLE, COUNSELS AND INSTRUCTS PERCEVAL

'TIS true, dear nephew. Now repent!
Have pity on your soul; intent,
If you are, on true repentance,
Then seek to go, in penitence,
To church, every day, in lieu
Of elsewhere, twill profit you.
Make sure you never fail to go
If you are in a place you know
Contains a church, or a chapel,
Go at the sounding of the bell;
If you've risen earlier, go then;
For how can it harm you, when
Your soul doth prosper if you go.
And if the mass has started, so
Much the better, stay till the priest
Is silent, and his chant has ceased.
If all this you do willingly,
If in this your spirit is free,
You may yet attain the prize,
And find a place in paradise.
Love God, believe in God, adore
Him; show all good folk honour;

And stand, when the priest is there,
For such demands but little care;
God loves that act, in verity,
Since it displays humility.
For all your sins in this place,
Do all, if you would win God's grace
Which you possessed, years ago.
Now tell me then, will you do so?'
'Yes, indeed, and most willingly.'
'Then I ask that you stay with me,
For two whole days, and do eat,
As a penance, but the food I eat.'
And Perceval to this agreed,
And the hermit in the Creed
Instructed him and, soft but clear,
Whispered a prayer in his ear,
Repeating it, till it remained.
And that prayer itself contained
A host of names of Our Lord,
The greatest language doth afford,
So powerful no mouth should name,
Except in fear of death, the same.
When he'd taught him the prayer,
He warned him to take great care
To speak it not, except in peril.
'Sire, I will not,' said Perceval.
So he remained, and so he heard
In joy, their service, every word,
And then to the cross he prayed,
And wept for his sins, and made
Obeisance, and repented humbly,
And thus, a lengthy while, knelt he.
That evening he sat down to eat
All the hermit was pleased to eat,
While his horse had a bed of straw,

'*And the hermit in the Creed*
Instructed him and, soft but clear'
Adapted from Le Morte d'Arthur (1893), Sir Thomas Malory
(15th cent) and Ernest Rhys (1859-1946)
Internet Archive Book Images

And barley and oats and, cared for
In a stable, was thus well-served,
Bathed and groomed, as he deserved.
Thus Perceval came to know again
That God, upon a Friday, was fain
To meet His death upon the cross;
At Easter-tide thus Perceval was
Granted communion, blamelessly.
Of Perceval's tale, more lengthily,
Here the book tells nary a word,
But you will certainly have heard
More than enough of Lord Gawain,
Ere I speak of Perceval again.

The End of the Tale of Perceval

TRANSLATOR'S AFTERWORD:

Chrétien's material concerning Perceval and the Grail finishes here, providing an artistically satisfying ending. His unfinished text continues, however, for a further three thousand lines or so, relating further adventures of Gawain, which are not directly pertinent to the Grail story, and do not mention Perceval. They should logically preface the four lengthy Continuations of the Grail story, penned by other medieval authors (Wauchier de Denain/Pseudo-Wauchier, Gerbert, and Manessier). Those who wish to know more of Gawain and Perceval, and of the Grail, should refer to the Continuation texts, of which English translations have been published. Suffice it to say that, in my humble opinion, Chrétien's tale is the first and the best, balancing Gawain, the exemplar of the courtly code of chivalry and courtesy, with the naïve Perceval, who ultimately follows the spiritual path. Note that Chrétien's patron, Philip I, Count of Flanders, died at the Siege of Acre in 1191 during the Third (and his second) Crusade, which may explain the tale's intertwining of the courtly and religious duties of knighthood.

ABOUT THE AUTHOR

Chrétien, likely a native of Troyes in north-eastern France, served at the court of his patroness, Marie of France, Countess of Champagne and daughter of Eleanor of Aquitaine, between 1160 and 1172. Hers was a literate court, and she herself knowledgeable in Latin as well as French texts, and Chrétien used the legendary court of King Arthur as an analogue for the French and Angevin courts of his own day. Marie's mother Eleanor became Queen of England, in 1154, as the spouse of Henry II, following annulment of her marriage to Louis VII of France, thus Chrétien was able to blend French and British traditions in his works. Between 1170 and 1190, Chrétien, writing in fluent octosyllabic couplets, developed and transformed the narrative verse tradition, and laid the foundations for the plot-driven prose narratives of later times.

ABOUT THE TRANSLATOR

Anthony Kline lives in England. He graduated in Mathematics from the University of Manchester, and was Chief Information Officer (Systems Director) of a large UK Company, before dedicating himself to his literary work and interests. He was born in 1947. His work consists of translations of poetry; critical works, biographical history with poetry as a central theme; and his own original poetry. He has translated into English from Latin, Ancient Greek, Classical Chinese and the European languages. He also maintains a deep interest in developments in Mathematics and the Sciences.

He continues to write predominantly for the Internet, making all works available in download format, with an added focus on the rapidly developing area of electronic books. His most extensive works are complete translations of Ovid's Metamorphoses and Dante's Divine Comedy.